WILLA CATHER

MODERN LITERATURE MONOGRAPHS

GENERAL EDITOR: Lina Mainiero

In the same series:

(Continued on last page of book)

WILLA CATHER

Dorothy Tuck McFarland

Frederick Ungar Publishing Co.
New York

Second Printing, 1978
Copyright © 1972 by Frederick Ungar Publishing Co., Inc.
Printed in the United States of America
Library of Congress Catalog Card Number: 74-190351
ISBN: 0-8044-2610-4 (cloth)

To the memory of
Adrienne Koch,
whose life was an inspiration
that endures

Contents

viii

Contents

Chronology

1873: 7 December: Willa Cather is born in the village of Back Creek (now Gore), near Winchester, Virginia.

1883: April: the family moves to her grandfather's homestead near Red Cloud, Nebraska.

1884: September: family moves to Red Cloud.

1891: September: enters the University of Nebraska.

1892: May: her first short story, "Peter," is published in the Boston magazine *The Mahogany Tree*. It is reprinted in the *Hesperian* in November.

1893: November: Willa Cather begins writing a column for the Nebraska State *Journal*.

1895: June: graduates from the University of Nebraska.

1896: June: moves to Pittsburgh to edit the *Home Monthly* magazine.

1897: September: begins work on the telegraph desk of the Pittsburgh *Leader*.

1898–99: Winter: meets Isabelle McClung.

1901: Spring: begins teaching Latin at Pittsburgh's Central High School and moves into McClung family house.

1902: June: Willa Cather makes her first trip to Europe.

1903: April: the volume of poems *April Twilights* is published.

1905:   The volume of short stories *The Troll Garden* is published.

1906:   May: Willa Cather moves to New York to work on *McClure's Magazine*.

1908:   Fall: takes an apartment with Edith Lewis at 82 Washington Place.

1911:   Fall: takes leave of absence from *McClure's*.

1912:   Her first novel, *Alexander's Bridge,* is published.

1913:   Moves into apartment at 5 Bank Street. The novel *O Pioneers!* is published.

1915:   The novel *The Song of the Lark* is published.

1917:   June: Willa Cather receives an honorary degree from the University of Nebraska. Summer: makes her first visit to Jaffrey, New Hampshire, where she will spend her autumns until 1938.

1918:   The novel *My Ántonia* is published.

1920:   The collection of short stories *Youth and the Bright Medusa* is published.

1922:   July: lectures at Breadloaf School, Middlebury, Vermont. The novel *One of Ours* is published. Willa Cather makes her first visit to Grand Manan Island, New Brunswick.

1923:   Receives the Pulitzer Prize for *One of Ours*. The novel *A Lost Lady* is published.

1925:   Builds summer cottage on Grand Manan Island. The novel *The Professor's House* is published.

1926:   The novel *My Mortal Enemy* is published.

1927:   The novel *Death Comes for the Archbishop* is published.

1928:   June: receives honorary degree from Columbia University.

1929:   June: receives honorary degree from Yale.

1930:   Receives gold medal of the American Academy of Arts and Letters for *Death Comes for the Archbishop*.

1931: Receives honorary degree from the University of California and honorary degree from Princeton University (the first to be awarded to a woman). The novel *Shadows on the Rock* is published.

1932: The collection of short stories *Obscure Destinies* is published. December: moves into apartment at 570 Park Avenue.

1933: Is awarded Prix Femina Américain for *Shadows on the Rock*. Receives honorary degree from Smith College.

1935: The novel *Lucy Gayheart* is published.

1936: The collection of literary criticism *Not under Forty* is published.

1937: Houghton Mifflin begins publishing the definitive edition of Willa Cather's works.

1940: The novel *Sapphira and the Slave Girl* is published.

1947: 24 April: Willa Cather dies of a cerebral hemorrhage in New York.

1948: The collection of short stories *The Old Beauty, and Others* is published.

1949: *On Writing* is published.

An Overview

On reading the biography and criticism written on Willa Cather, one is struck with the variety of responses to her both as a personality and a writer. From the testimonies of those who knew her, especially her friends Edith Lewis and Elizabeth Sergeant, she emerges as a warm, attractive personality, strong-willed, capable of deep friendships, loyal, self-confident, generous. In contast to this is the image of the older Willa Cather as an embittered and petty old woman who shut herself away from a modern world she intensely disliked. This interpretation of her led so eminent a critic as Lionel Trilling to suggest that her "self-conscious and defiant . . . rejection of her own time must make her talent increasingly irrelevant and tangential—for any time."[1]

A recent tendency has been to see in Willa Cather's work veiled and perhaps even unconscious reconstructions of her own personal anxieties and traumas. Thus, John Randall has largely interpreted her work in terms of what he feels was her failure to reach emotional maturity, her yearning backward to a vanished youth, a vanished era. Leon Edel saw *The Professor's House* as a thinly disguised description of Willa Cather's despair over the marriage of her long-time friend Isabelle McClung to Jan Hambourg, reputedly the model for Louie Marsellus in that novel, and identifies the professor's attic study-cum-sewing-room, which he is so loath to leave, with the attic study in the McClung's Pittsburgh house, where Willa Cather worked for so many years.

Willa Cather's most recent biographer, James Woodress, has generally followed Mr. Edel's interpretation in stressing the depth of the relationship between Willa Cather and Isabelle and the shock and distress that Willa Cather suffered at Isabelle's marriage. He relates this to the "over-all note of death, defeat, frustration, and loss" that began to be sounded in *Youth and the Bright Medusa* (1920) and continued through *My Mortal Enemy* (1926).[2]

Willa Cather was reticent about her private life. She refused to allow her letters to be published (though many of them may be read and are deposited in various libraries), she disliked publicity, and she was unwilling to become a public figure even though she was a great popular and critical success. Her reticence has undoubtedly contributed to this critical eagerness to penetrate her reserve, to find out the "truth" by subjecting what evidence she did leave behind to a kind of psychoanalysis, the results of which seem, at best, to be mildly discrediting and to explain away more than they explain. Her inevitable human failings, her weaknesses, her difficulties, the life problems she undoubtedly struggled with, probably are reflected in her work to some extent, but they are not the whole of it. Too much emphasis on this type of speculative biography seems to me to remove the focus from her writing as art that points beyond itself and redirects our attention to the fallible human being who produced it.

At her best, Willa Cather was capable of great artistry; this no one denies. Her art lies primarily in her power to create with words vivid pictorial images that are imbued with an ineffable quality of felt reality, and her narrative technique is essentially a juxtaposition of many images which work together to produce a cumulative effect and suggest something more than what is literally said, which evokes a feeling, a mood, or a quality of character. Her style is remarkable for its clarity and deceptive simplicity. Her use of words as a medium to convey images is so skillful that the words become almost transparent; images are conveyed to one's mind so immediately that one has little sense of the fine craftsmanship of the prose with which they are built.

It is not her artistry, then, that is in question, but the content of her works. Some critics have argued that the most prominent theme in her work, the celebration of the past and of traditional values, however beautifully treated, makes her work, as Trilling so devastatingly said of it, irrelevant. Alfred Kazin, a generally sympathetic critic, accepts Willa Cather's right to her traditionalism but clearly stands apart from it himself. He discusses her traditionalism as "a candid and philosophical nostalgia," the very intensity of which "had given her the conviction that the values of the world she had lost were the primary values, and everything else merely their degradation."[3]

Here, I think, is the real core of the controversy over Willa Cather: the question of values. Kazin, who admires her as an artist, pronounces her values to be

"exquisitely futile."[4] "Elegiac" and "nostalgic" are
words often used to describe her work, acknowledging
again the attractiveness of the past of which she wrote,
but also implying the impossibility of the past serving
any longer as a model in the modern world. Kazin and
others suggest that she demonstrated in her own life
the failure of traditionalism,. and in *A Lost Lady* and
The Professor's House "submitted her art almost re-
joicingly to the subtle exploration of failure."[5] Yet
these "explorations of failure" are followed by her
masterpiece, *Death Comes for the Archbishop,* in
which order, hierarchy, tradition, ritual as the basis for
a whole and meaningful life, are triumphantly celebrated.

All of what Willa Cather wrote, it seems to me, is
ultimately a metaphor of the conflict which Miguel de
Unamuno referred to as an "inward tragedy," the conflict "between what the world is as scientific reason
shows it to be, and what we wish it might be, as our
religious faith affirms it to be."[6] For Willa Cather, this
conflict was most broadly expressed in terms of the
world she knew in her childhood—the pioneer era
which she clearly idealized and ennobled in her fictional re-creation of it—and the post-World War I
wasteland she so thoroughly repudiated. It is easy to
lose sight of the essentially symbolic nature of this conflict and to read it too narrowly in terms of literal past
versus literal present. Her theme was not the superiority of the past over the present, but, as Henry Steele
Commager has observed, "the supremacy of moral and
spiritual over material values, the ever recurrent but
inexhaustible theme of gaining the whole world and
losing one's soul."[7] Rather than being irrelevant to the
modern world, the moral thrust of Willa Cather's art,

her concern with pioneers and artists as symbolic figures representing the unending human quest for
beauty and truth, places her among the number, not of
the backward-looking (which she saw herself as being
one of), but of the true spiritual pioneers of all ages in
whose lives or work other men continue to find inspiration. Unamuno might have been speaking of
Willa Cather when he wrote:

. . . everyone who fights for any ideal whatever, although
his ideal may seem to lie in the past, is driving the world on
to the future, and . . . the only reactionaries are those who
find themselves at home in the present. Every supposed res-
toration of the past is a creation of the future, and if the
past which it is sought to restore is a dream, something im-
perfectly known, so much the better. The march, as ever, is
towards the future, and he who marches is getting there,
even though he march walking backwards. And who knows
if that is not the better way! . . .[8]

1

Willa Cather's Life

Though usually identified with the Nebraska setting of her pioneer novels, Willa Cather was not a native midwesterner. She was born on 7 December 1873 near Winchester, Virginia, in the village of Back Creek (now named Gore), where she lived until she was nine years old. In 1883 her family moved to her grandfather's farm on the Nebraska frontier, about twenty miles west of Red Cloud. Because her mother's health was poor, Willa was left largely to her own devices. She spent her time discovering the prairie, riding about the countryside on her pony, and visiting the struggling immigrants from Norway, from Sweden, and from Bohemia in their dugouts and sod houses. She did not go to school, but in the evenings she read aloud to her grandmother from the English classics, the Bible, and *Pilgrim's Progress.*

In September 1884 her family moved to Red Cloud. In these first years in Nebraska, Willa Cather absorbed what was to become much of the material of her later fiction. Those years gave her the background for *O Pioneers!* and *My Ántonia,* and Red Cloud was to become the model for virtually all the western towns in her writing.

She was almost eleven years old when she first began to go to school. She had good teachers in Red Cloud, and she was fortunate in finding several unusual adult friends whose intellectual or artistic interests stimulated her own developing mind. William Ducker, an Englishman, who was a lover of the classics, began to tutor Willa in Latin and Greek when she was in her early teens. She took piano lessons from Professor Shindelmeisser, a talented musician with an unfortunate tendency to drink. He was to become the model for Professor Wunsch in *The Song of the Lark.* She was introduced to European literature in the home of her neighbors Mr. and Mrs. Wiener, a cultivated German Jewish couple who appear as the Rosens in "Old Mrs. Harris."

Young Willa Cather was clearly an unusual girl in Red Cloud. She liked the companionship of immigrants and of older people with intellectual tastes. She dressed like her brothers, and in her teens she had her hair cut short like a boy. She made friends with the town doctors and went out on their rounds with them into the countryside, on at least one occasion assisting at an emergency surgery.

At sixteen Willa Cather left Red Cloud for the Latin school in Lincoln, where she studied a year before entering the University of Nebraska. Late in 1893 she began a regular Sunday column of "sketches, observations, and theatrical and literary comment"[1] in the Nebraska State *Journal.* "The Passing Show," as the column was called, appeared from 1893 until the spring of 1900. She also began writing play reviews for the *Journal,* which soon were marked by distinctiveness and style, as well as by trenchant and sometimes devastating criticism.

Together these columns and reviews constitute almost a journal of what Willa Cather was reading, seeing, and thinking about during her college years, and they are an invaluable record of her explorations of the meaning of art and the nature of the artist. The prose is vivid, vigorous, sure, sometimes crisp, sometimes exalted and incantatory, always written with feeling and carrying within it the quality of the author's personal voice. Again and again she expressed a concern with the unfathomable mystery of art, and she attempted to plumb its depths. Again and again she found at the root of art the ability to feel deeply and to make others feel. By "feeling" she meant not mere sensation, not even sensitivity, but an awareness of the deepest levels of reality, which the artist first experiences himself and then re-creates for others through the medium of his creative imagination. She did not disparage or discount the intellect, but she insisted on the primacy of the imagination. For her, imagination was the creative power of the artist, the closest approximation on the human level to the creative power of divinity. The artist, then, becomes the transmitter of ultimate truth, ultimate reality. It was to take Willa Cather another thirty years to achieve in her fiction "those moments of absolute reality of experience"[2] that she recognized as the touchstone of art; but even at the very beginning of her writing career she was aware of her goal.

After Willa Cather graduated from the university she remained in Lincoln for a year, writing for the *Journal* and the *Courier,* a newly reorganized weekly newspaper. In 1896 she moved to Pittsburgh, working first at the *Home Monthly* magazine, then on the Pittsburgh *Daily Leader*.

While in Pittsburgh she met Isabelle McClung, the daughter of a prominent judge. Isabelle responded at once to Willa Cather's "warm, frank, radiantly outgoing nature . . . her artistic gifts, the sureness and fire of her approach to life and ideas."[3] Though not an artist herself, Isabelle was a devotee of the arts, and she found in Willa Cather "the key to everything she herself was seeking." A deep friendship that was to last a lifetime developed between the two women. In the spring of 1901 Isabelle fixed up an attic sewing room as a study for Willa and invited her to live in the

McClung home. There, in the companionship of a lit-
erate, sympathetic friend, amid the domestic comforts
of a wealthy household, Willa Cather spent the next
five years, returning frequently for long visits after she
had left Pittsburgh to move to New York.

Early in 1900 Willa Cather left the *Daily Leader*.
After a year of writing stories and working briefly as
a government translator in Washington, she returned
to Pittsburgh and taught at Pittsburgh's Central High
School. In the summer of 1902 she traveled to Europe
with Isabelle McClung. (The accounts of this trip
appeared in 1956 under the title *Willa Cather in
Europe*.)

Willa Cather's first published book, a volume of
poems called *April Twilights,* appeared in 1903. These
poems, which received a number of favorable reviews,
showed considerable skill in the handling of a variety
of metrical schemes, and the conventional sentiments
of the poems are expressed with deftness. But one
misses the "individual voice" that she later spoke of
as a criterion of the true artist.

Like her poetry, which, though skillful, was de-
rivative, Willa Cather's first volume of short stories,
The Troll Garden (1905), showed the influence of the
successful writers of the day, especially that of Henry
James. The stories are meticulously constructed, each
dealing in a different way with the allure and the dangers of the world of culture and art, to which the "troll
garden" metaphor of the title refers. The much-
anthologized "Paul's Case" is a small masterpiece of
sustained tone. Willa Cather presented Paul with dis-
passionate clarity: constricted, tense, tormented by a
groping desire for beauty but taken in by mere tinsel
and stage properties. She also regarded him with deep

compassion, and it is in the counterpoint of these two attitudes that the story gains its strength. Paul may be taken in by illusion, but Willa Cather re-creates Paul's delight in his illusory experience so powerfully that the reader, too, is caught up in the magic of Paul's fantasies.

In 1906 Willa Cather left Pittsburgh to join the staff of *McClure's Magazine* in New York, becoming managing editor in the spring of 1909. She continued to write, finishing her first novel, *Alexander's Bridge,* in the fall of 1911. She was later to be very critical of this novel, saying that its construction and its upper-class setting were imitative and contrived, written out of a young writer's inability to distinguish between "his own material and that which he would like to make his own."[4] But she recognized that her choice of sophisticated subject matter, however mistaken, was part of the normal course of development, a phase that one goes through on one's journey to find himself:

I think usually the young writer must have his affair with the external material he covets; must imitate and strive to follow the masters he most admires, until he finds he is starving for reality and cannot make this go any longer. Then he learns that it is not the adventure he sought, but the adventure that sought him, which has made the enduring mark upon him.[5]

With the completion of *Alexander's Bridge,* Willa Cather had accomplished the tasks of her apprenticeship. The girl from the Nebraska prairie had lived in a sophisticated, urban society; she had proved herself as a successful editor of one of New York's leading magazines; she had traveled in Europe; she had known cultivated and famous people. Now thirty-eight, she had made her mark on the world but found herself "starving for reality." She was ready at last to follow the advice given her nearly three years before by the New England writer Sarah Orne Jewett, who had written her that, to progress as a writer, she should free herself from the demands of her work at *McClure's* and find her "own quiet centre of life and write from that."[6]

Thus, in the fall of 1911 Willa Cather took a leave of absence from *McClure's* and, with Isabelle McClung, rented a house in Cherry Valley, New York. Here she wrote a novella, "The Bohemian Girl," set among immigrant families in Nebraska. In this novella Willa Cather was writing of the land and people she knew best. The result is a piece of work that is clear in style, with vivid, realistic dialogue and deft, sharp characterizations. It has the unmistakable feel of reality about it. The descriptive writing is strong and sure, and one scene especially—the barn-raising party—is reminiscent of the work of the Flemish painters; it has the same warmth and depth and light, and the crowded canvas filled with individual portraits, ruddy, glowing with unself-conscious life. In terms of narrative power and evocation of feeling, "The Bohemian Girl" is far superior to anything Willa Cather had written up to that time.

In the early spring of 1912 Willa Cather set off on a journey to visit her brother Douglass in Winslow, Arizona. From April to June she absorbed the vast, splendid light and space of the southwest, traveling over the country from Santa Fe and Albuquerque to the Grand Canyon and a canyon of the Little Colorado in which there were cliff dwellings. She made the acquaintance of a Catholic priest in Winslow and went out with him on his visits to distant parishes; from him she learned much of the legends and history of the country and its Spanish and Indian people. Her brother had many friends among the Mexicans who lived on the other side of the railroad tracks. Willa Cather, too, responded to the warmth and spontaneity of the Mexicans and made friends with three musicians and a handsome singer, who often came to play and sing for her. The young singer, especially, delighted her with his simplicity and natural piety; being with him, she felt, "was like living in a classic age."[7]

Though she did no writing at all during this visit, the impressions made on her by the country, its people, and its history were obviously deep—indeed, it was to become the deepest and richest source of writing that she would discover during her adult life.

Willa Cather's work written in the years from 1913 to 1920 falls into two main categories: the poetic, evocative, one might even say heroic novels (*O Pioneers!* and *My Antonia*) set in the pioneer past; and the more realistic, present-oriented works dealing with the conflict between the artist and his world (the novel *The Song of the Lark* and the short stories in *Youth and the Bright Medusa*).

In her fifth novel, *One of Ours,* on which she worked from 1918 to 1922, she combined the prairie setting of the pioneer novels with her concerns about the contemporary world. What she had expressed earlier as the conflict between the artist and his world appears in *One of Ours* embodied in a Nebraska farm boy whose innocence and idealism. make him a misfit in a materialistic and shallow society. Willa Cather was gravely disturbed by the growth of materialism, by the rise of machine technology, which alienated man from the land and which made possible the heretofore un-dreamed-of destructiveness of World War I. She felt very deeply the spiritual dislocation and disillusion-ment of the postwar years, which in one way or an-other affected every significant author writing during the 1920s. She was not yet able, however, to translate these concerns into a work of art, and *One of Ours* is one of her less successful novels.

Willa Cather continued to explore the conflict between materialism and idealism, but she developed the ability to do so more indirectly and far more suc-cessfully. Her next three novels are all variously ren-dered expressions of conflict: the conflict between the ennobling values of the pioneer era and the dehuman-ization of the present in *A Lost Lady* (1923); the con-flict between a spiritual man and a materialistic society in *The Professor's House* (1925); and finally, the con-flict between the mortal longings of the flesh for worldly beauty and love and the desire of the soul for immortality in *My Mortal Enemy* (1926).

A sense of the sacred, especially as revealed in na-ture, is evident in Willa Cather's work as early as *O Pioneers!* and *My Ántonia.* In 1922 she converted to the Episcopal faith. Critics have tended to play down her conversion, saying that her interest in religion was primarily aesthetic. But to say (as does the protagonist in *The Professor's House*) that religion and art are, in the end, the same thing is not necessarily to regard them both as aesthetic experiences: it is also a way of saying that both are means of approaching absolute reality. Though the religious elements of *The Profes-sor's House* and *My Mortal Enemy* are presented in an ambiguous light, it is clear that Willa Cather was con-cerned with ultimate questions and ultimate values, and with the conflict, in contemporary times, between these and secular values.

Perhaps feeling that this conflict could not be resolved in the present, Willa Cather turned again to the past for the setting of her next novel, *Death Comes for the Archbishop* (1927), in which the civilizing values of the Catholic faith are engrafted onto the half-pagan world of the Mexican and Indian southwest. *Shadows on the Rock*, which followed in 1931, is another expression of the same theme: the establishment of French Catholicism and culture in the savage wilderness of seventeenth-century Quebec.

The years following the publication of *Death Comes for the Archbishop* were years of increased recognition of Willa Cather's important position in American letters. She was awarded honorary degrees from Columbia, Yale, the University of California, and Princeton, and the gold medal of the American Academy of Arts and Letters. They were also years, however, in which she suffered deep personal losses. Her father, to whom she had always been close, died early in 1928, and her mother suffered a paralytic stroke in 1929 and died in 1931.

The deaths of her parents drew Willa Cather back to memories of her childhood and of her family, out of which grew the short stories in *Obscure Destinies* (1932) and, later, the novel *Sapphira and the Slave Girl* (1940), which she began in 1937.

During the years 1935 to 1937 Willa Cather was occupied with preparing a collection of her critical writings and a definitive edition of her fiction. Her critical work, which appeared in 1936, was entitled *Not under Forty*. It was in the preface to this book that she made the often-quoted remark that "the world broke in two in 1922 or thereabouts," and emphatically

linked herself with those over forty who could identify
with the world as it was before 1922. The book is not
nearly so reactionary as this declaration might lead one
to expect. The essays "The Novel Démeublé," *"Joseph
and His Brothers,"* and "Katherine Mansfield" pertain
very much to the present. Though the subjects of the
three remaining essays belong more to the nineteenth
century than the twentieth—Mme. Franklin Grout (the
niece of Gustave Flaubert) of "A Chance Meeting";
Mrs. James T. Fields, hostess of Boston's greatest literary salon, of "148 Charles Street"; and Sarah Orne
Jewett of "Miss Jewett"—the feelings and literary opinions are timeless. There are passages here and there
that reflect Willa Cather's feeling that the modern
world had cut itself off from its roots in the past. This
feeling might have been partly personal chagrin, as at
the fact that a garage now occupies the site of Mrs.
Fields's home at 148 Charles Street, but it also stemmed
from an awareness of the great cultural loss that such
a chance so graphically symbolizes.

Though a romantic in the priority she gave to
feeling ("in novels, as in poetry, the facts are nothing,
the feeling is everything"),[8] Willa Cather was a classi-
cist in her respect for the past as the guardian of
proved values; Mrs. Fields's drawing room represented
to her "the peace of the past, where the tawdry and
cheap have been eliminated and the enduring things
have taken their proper, happy places."[9] Throughout
the essays runs the thread of her concern with excel-
lence, with the whole legacy of Western civilization
that stands on the far side of 1922 as opposed to what
seemed to her to be a spiritually impoverished present.

Perhaps the most interesting critical theme in the
collection is Willa Cather's analysis of the process of
creation: how a writer makes something "that belongs

to Literature" as distinct from "merely a good story."[10]
She approached the core of her concern from different
angles: art is not the result of mere literalness or veri-
similitude, of putting down on paper all that registers
on one's senses; nor, in the other extreme, is it a matter
of the writer improving upon his material "by using
his 'imagination' upon it and twisting it to suit his
purpose."[11] The subject matter of art, she suggested,
must have its own integrity, its own qualities of enduring worth, which are indicated by its "persistence, survival, recurrence in the writer's mind."[12] Given this,
the actual translating of the subject matter into art
involves an attitude toward his material that allows the
writer to see it clearly, to see the human reality which
must infuse the story if it is to be of enduring value.
The writer must give himself absolutely to his material, and "this gift of sympathy . . . is the fine thing
in him that alone can make his work fine."[13] To bor-
row a modern term, one might say that art depends on
the authenticity of both the subject matter and the
writer's response to it. This is surely a valid criterion,
and one which the best of Willa Cather's own fiction
fulfills admirably.

At the time of her death, Willa Cather left unfin-
ished a novel set in medieval Avignon on which she
had been working fitfully since 1942, handicapped by
an inflamed tendon in her wrist that made writing
difficult and sometimes impossible. In accordance with
the terms of her will, the manuscript was destroyed.
She died of a cerebral hemorrhage on 24 April 1947
and was buried at Jaffrey, New Hampshire, where she
had spent the autumns between 1918 and 1938. Carved
on her tombstone are lines from *My Ántonia*:

. . . That is happiness; to be dissolved into something complete and great.

2

O Pioneers!

(1913)

When she returned to Red Cloud from her visit to the southwest in 1912, Willa Cather found in her mind a story, which was to be called "The White Mulberry Tree," and a poem called "Prairie Spring." With the new story she juxtaposed another story written the winter before in Cherry Valley, "Alexandra." This "two-part pastoral," after considerable additions linking and clarifying the relationships of the two stories, became *O Pioneers!* The poem, which is in essence the poetic distillation of *O Pioneers!*, she placed at the beginning of the novel.

With *O Pioneers!* Willa Cather was "suddenly in control of inner creative forces which had tended to swamp her and make her dismal so long as she could not use them."[1] She was writing for herself, about people she knew—"some Scandinavians and Bohemians who had been neighbours of ours when I . . . was eight or nine years old."[2] The story had welled up in her: "there was no arranging or 'inventing'; everything was spontaneous and took its own place, right or wrong."[3] But she did not expect much to come of it; it was too unconventional.

I ignored all the situations and accents that were then generally thought to be necessary. The "novel of the soil" had not then come into fashion in this country. The drawing-room was considered the proper setting for a novel, and the only characters worth reading about were smart people or clever people. . . . I did not in the least expect that other people would see anything in a slow-moving story, without "action," without "humour," without a "hero"; a story concerned entirely with heavy farming people, with cornfields and pasture lands and pig yards—set in Nebraska, of all places![4]

20

Though the Nebraska setting of *O Pioneers!* was, at the time of its writing, unconventional, its themes are classic and universal. It deals with the two or three human stories that "go on repeating themselves as fiercely as if they had never happened before; like the larks . . . that have been singing the same five notes for thousands of years" (p. 119).* The novel's basic theme, the pioneer story of taming and making fruitful the wild prairie, is the background against which are set the more personal but thematically similar stories of love, birth, and death—the basic realities of man's existence.

Part I, "The Wild Land," which deals with the pioneer experience, stresses the importance of the relationship of man to the land. The novel opens on the raw, barren countryside óf winter; against the savage vastness of the untamed land men seem weak and puny, their houses dwarfed, their roads only faint tracks in the grass. Having struggled to wrest a living from the wild land for eleven years, John Bergson lies dying, willing to pass on the struggle to his strong daughter, Alexandra. Bergson exemplifies one possible relationship to the land—that of impersonal ownership —which is shown, by its results, to be inadequate. Other characters in this section embody other possible attitudes. Six months after the death of her father, Alexandra and her brothers and her good friend Carl Linstrum go to visit Crazy Ivar, a queer old Norwegian who lives close to nature with the simplicity of a wild creature. Deeply religious, he explains that he prefers his way of life apart from people and at one with na-

* Page references in this discussion are to *O Pioneers!* (Boston: Houghton Mifflin Co., 1913).

ture by saying that "his Bible seemed truer to him
there."

> If one stood in the doorway of his cave, and looked off at
> the rough land, the smiling sky, the curly grass white in the
> hot sunlight; if one listened to the rapturous song of the
> lark, the drumming of the quail, the burr of the locust
> against that vast silence, one understood what Ivar meant
> [p. 38].

While to John Bergson the land was an impersonal force against which man pitted his strength only
to die, to Crazy Ivar, as to the Psalmist, it is transparent to the glory of God. Alexandra responds to Ivar,
seeking his advice on the care of her hogs; but to her
stolid and unimaginative brothers, Oscar and Lou,
who have no love of nature and view their farm merely
as a way of making a living, Ivar is simply crazy and
possibly dangerous.

The ideal of man's creative relationship to the
land is personified in Alexandra. This is dramatized
three years later, when drought and crop failure
threaten to drive the settlers out. Carl Linstrum and
his family leave. Thus Alexandra is deprived of her
closest friend, the only person who really understands
her. Oscar and Lou, too, want to sell out, and they
angrily oppose Alexandra, whose deep faith in the
future of the land convinces her that this is the time
to buy all the land they can. She decides to take the
wagon and travel with her youngest brother, eight-
year-old Emil, to the farms to the south, along the
river, to see how things are going there. On her return
she renews her faith that the Divide, the high plateau
country, will yield to being cultivated and become rich
farmland, and she fortifies her determination to remain.

When the road began to climb the first long swells of the
Divide, Alexandra hummed an old Swedish hymn, and Emil
wondered why his sister looked so happy. Her face was so
radiant that he felt shy about asking her. For the first time,
perhaps, since that land emerged from the waters of geologic ages, a human face was set toward it with love and
yearning. It seemed beautiful to her, rich and strong and
glorious. Her eyes drank in the breadth of it, until her tears
blinded her. Then the Genius of the Divide, the great, free
spirit which breathes across it, must have bent lower than it
ever bent to a human will before. The history of every
country begins in the heart of a man or a woman [p. 65].

Though many have attempted to subdue the land,
its submission to the hand of man is dependent on love
rather than force. As the settlement of a wild land is
symbolically equivalent to the divine act of creation,
which established an ordered universe out of primordial chaos,[5] it is an undertaking which is charged with
significance for the entire community. Right relationship with the land produces right order. Thus, Alexandra's relationship to the land not only brings the
land under submission to the plow and makes it fruitful; it also brings into being, in Alexandra's household,
a human community which is ordered and harmonious,
and whose harmoniousness depends on the continu-
ance of right relationships among its members.

Part II, "Neighboring Fields," shifts the focus
from man's relationship to the land to the human
community. As in Part I Alexandra's creative response
to the land is symbolically parallel to the Creation,
Part II opens on a scene that is faintly suggestive of
Eden, but which already contains foreshadowings of
the Fall—the breaking of right order—and of death,
which is its consequence. Thus, against the placid back-

ground of the fertile and prosperous Divide, Alexandra's brother Emil, now a young man of twenty-one just home from college, is scything the grass in the graveyard where his father and mother are buried. Marie Shabata drives by in her carriage and offers Emil a ride home to Alexandra's farm, which is one of the richest on the Divide. The scenes that follow reinforce the contrast between the way of life that grows out of Alexandra's relationship with the land and that of her materialistic brothers. Alexandra has invited Crazy Ivar to live with her because he lost his land, and she employs three Swedish girls to help her in the house and six men to work the farm. Lou and Oscar, now married and on farms of their own, still criticize her forward-looking ways of farming and grumble that Ivar is dangerous and should be put in an asylum. Alexandra's openness to things of value in both the old and the new—her sympathy and understanding of the needs of Ivar and of the old-fashioned Mrs. Lee, Lou's mother-in-law, and her willingness to try alfalfa or a silo when none of her neighbors would hear of such a thing—are implicitly contrasted with her brothers' slavery to conventional ways of behavior and their concern over what people might say.

Carl Linstrum unexpectedly returns, stopping for a visit en route to Alaska, where he intends to try prospecting for gold. Oscar and Lou despise him because they believe he has never amounted to much. Artistic and sensitive, he has left his profession as an engraver because he cares about fine wood engravings, and all that is being done now is cheap metal work. Through Carl, the pettiness and conventionality of Alexandra's brothers is seen as a metaphor of the lack of right order in the world at large, where modern prosperity has brought not only relative ease and abundance but shallowness and lack of taste and scorn of those who cannot or will not follow the conventional patterns of behavior.

Chapter five returns to the theme of death suggested by the figure of Emil scything the grass in the graveyard in the opening pages of Part II, and introduces an image of death as the outcome of the thoughtless pursuit of desire. Carl, out for an early morning walk to visit his old farm, now owned by the irascible, jealous Frank Shabata and his pretty wife, Marie, unintentionally observes Marie and Emil looking for ducks on the pond. Emil shoots and brings the dead birds back to Marie, whose delight changes to despair when she sees what her careless joy in pursuing the birds with Emil has done. This image prefigures the fate of Emil and Marie, which will be developed in the later section "The White Mulberry Tree."

The love stories within the human community are thematically parallel to Alexandra's loving response to the Divide, for both reflect the reaching out of the human heart toward beauty and the fullness of life. But the love between Emil and Marie, however powerful and alluring, is at variance with the order of the community, and the results of their love, from the very beginning, are disruptive, for Marie is another man's wife. The contrast between this frustrated love, which makes Emil harsh and quarrelsome, and the delight of harmonious love is emphasized in the portrayal of the happy, sunny love between Emil's best friend, Amédée, and his bride, Angélique. While Emil's love threatens right relationships within the community, the emerging and appropriate love between Carl and Alexandra is threatened by Alexandra's self-seeking brothers. Oscar and Lou fear that Carl will get her property, which they feel by right, if not by law, to be theirs. The section closes on a note of discord: Emil, determined to go away to Mexico, is blind to Alexandra's distress about Carl, and the formerly close relationship between brother and sister is at least temporarily broken. There is an open, angry breach between Alexandra and her other two brothers; Carl, unable to face the criticism of Lou and Oscar, unhappily decides that he must leave. Alexandra feels that all at once, in a single day, she has lost everything.

In Part IV, "The White Mulberry Tree," Emil returns to the Divide after a year in Mexico and is fatefully thrown together with Marie at a church festival. They are both miserable at the impossibility of their relationship, and Marie begs Emil to go away again. He packs his things and plans to leave for Omaha to read law. Before he can depart his best friend, Amédée, is stricken with appendicitis and dies. The next day, torn apart by grief and love, Emil leaves a gathering attended by Marie's husband and rides back to Marie to tell her good-by. He finds her alone in the orchard, dreaming of him. Several hours later, her rash and jealous husband returns and finds Emil's horse in the stable and the house dark. More to increase his sense of injury and self-importance than out of intention to kill anyone, he takes his gun and goes out searching for them. When he hears them behind the orchard hedge he blindly fires at them and then flees, terror-stricken at what he has done. He leaves Emil dead and Marie dying.

Through this act of violence, the placid Eden which Alexandra has created, in large part for Emil to inherit, is destroyed, and Alexandra herself symbolically undergoes the experience of death. As the last section opens, Alexandra is caught in a rainstorm at the graveyard. There, cold and soaking wet, she feels that the rain falling on her takes her back into the dark, before she was born. Brought home and put to bed, she feels tired of life, tired of her own aching body, and longs to be free. Then she experiences "the old illusion of her girlhood, of being lifted and carried lightly by someone very strong."

He was with her a long while this time, and carried her very far, and in his arms she felt free from pain. When he laid her down on the bed again, she opened her eyes, and, for the first time in her life, she saw him, saw him clearly, though the room was dark, and his face was covered. . . . His right arm, bared from the elbow, was dark and gleaming, like bronze, and she knew at once that it was the arm of the mightiest of all lovers. She knew at last for whom it was she had waited, and where he would carry her. That, she told herself, was very well. Then she went to sleep [pp. 282–83].

Some critics identify this "mightiest of all lovers" as death, but it should be remembered that he had appeared to her earlier as a personification of a god of vegetation, a god of corn, "yellow like the sunlight," who carried Alexandra in his arms "like a sheaf of wheat" (p. 206). Perhaps it would be more accurate to see him as a symbol of the life force itself, life that contains both fertility and death. Significantly, it is in her total acceptance of him—symbolically, her acceptance of death *and* life—that Alexandra finds peace. Strengthened by this experience, she determines to go to the state penitentiary to visit Frank Shabata.

The visit to Frank is a kind of descent into hell, and never has Alexandra seemed less armed with

power, more tired and worn, than she appears in the
prison. She enters into the depths of negation and
despair with Frank, herself taking on the burden of
his disgust with life in order to try to set him free.
There is no joy for her in this act, no feeling of pious
self-sacrifice; it is a painful task that leaves her spiritually exhausted, feeling that she has not much more life
in her than he. Only then, when she has reached the
bottom, does she receive a telegram saying that Carl
is returning, and life begins to flow into her again.

Alexandra's ascent from death is facilitated through
the love of Carl, who, the moment he learned of Alexandra's misfortune, had left his prospecting business
in Alaska and rushed to her as fast as trains and boats
could carry him. His earlier timidity in the face of her
brothers' disapproval vanishes in the awareness of her
need for him, and her grief has opened in her a greater
awareness of that need. Through Carl and Alexandra
the human stories are brought again into the larger
perspective and seen in relationship both with the passage of human history and with the land, the source
from which the actors spring and to which they must
return. At the close of the novel, the land theme wells
up, larger than all the human actors who have emerged
from it, but enriched by their lives as they are sustained by the land that bears them and which will
someday receive them "into its bosom, to give them out
again in the yellow wheat, in the rustling corn, in the
shining eyes of youth!" (p. 309).

3

The Song

of the Lark

(1915)

Taken by itself, *The Song of the Lark* is a skillful and intelligent narrative of the development of an artist, the singer Thea Kronborg, from her childhood in a little Colorado town to the pinnacle of her success in singing Wagnerian roles at the Metropolitan Opera. Compared to *O Pioneers!*, however, *The Song of the Lark* is disappointing. The spiritual core of the novel —Thea's discovery of the ultimate nature of art—is buried in a great mass of extraneous materialistic detail that describes her progress but does little to illuminate the inner nature of her quest. Willa Cather herself was dissatisfied with the novel after it was published, revising and cutting it extensively for the 1932 edition. At that time she also added a preface in which she suggested that the fault of the novel lay in its going on too long: "the life of a successful artist in the full tide of achievement is not so interesting as the life of a talented young girl 'fighting her way,' as we say" (p. v).*

The life of the American opera singer Olive Fremstad provided the skeletal framework of the novel. Born in Sweden, brought to Minnesota as a child, she grew up "in a new crude country where there was neither artistic stimulus nor discriminating taste. She was poor, and always had to earn her own living."[1] Miss Fremstad studied in Germany in her early twenties, and at thirty she began to sing at the Metropolitan Opera. Similarly, Willa Cather's Thea Kronborg, the child of Swedish parents, grew up in a "new, crude country," in a little town called Moonstone set at the edge of the desert, and, like Miss Fremstad, "fought her

* Page references in this discussion are to *The Song of the Lark,* new edition with preface (Boston: Houghton Mifflin Co., 1932).

own way toward the intellectual centers of the world," to Germany, and finally to the Metropolitan stage in New York. The details of Thea's life, however, especially the childhood scenes of Book I, are drawn from Willa Cather's own experience.

As a girl of as yet undifferentiated promise, Thea lives in an ordinary, crowded family and is remarkable largely for her friendships: with the town doctor, Howard Archie; a railroad man named Ray Kennedy; her music teacher, Professor Wunsch; the Kohlers, a German immigrant couple; and a volatile Mexican named Spanish Johnny. When Ray Kennedy—who had hoped to marry Thea when she was old enough—is killed in a railroad accident, Thea finds herself the beneficiary of his life insurance and with this money is enabled to go to Chicago to study music. In Chicago she studies piano until, almost accidentally, her piano teacher discovers her singing ability and urges her to study voice rather than piano. Discouraged and frustrated with her progress, she is rescued by the advent of Fred Ottenburg, a dashing and musically sophisticated heir to a large fortune, who makes it his avocation to further Thea's faltering career and liberate what he senses to be a remarkable talent.

In order to raise Thea out of her depression of body and spirit, Fred sends her to a ranch owned by his family in Arizona. On the ranch property are the cliff dwellings in Panther Canyon, and in the empty houses of the Ancient People Thea spends her days. The desert air, the light, the silence, and most of all the invisible presence of the Ancient People bring her to a state of patient waiting, and a feeling of receptivity replaces her previous frustrated striving. Thus attuned, one morning while bathing in the canyon stream she

comes to a recognition of the meaning of art; as the
Indian women had made jars to hold the precious
water—the source of life in an arid land—Thea sees all
art as

> an effort to make a sheath, a mould in which to imprison for
> a moment the shining, elusive element which is life itself,—
> life hurrying past us and running away, too strong to stop,
> too sweet to lose. . . . The Indian women had held it in
> their jars. . . . In singing, one made a vessel of one's throat
> and nostrils and held it on one's breath, caught the stream
> in a scale of natural intervals" [p. 304].

When she has made this discovery, she realizes
what she intends to do with her life, and she determines to go to Germany to study at the first opportu-
nity. Meanwhile, Fred Ottenburg joins her at the ranch
and persuades her to travel with him to Mexico City,
wanting to marry her and intending to help her career
in every possible way. Fred, however, is already married; he loathes his wife and is separated from her, but
she will not divorce him. When Thea learns this she
refuses further help from Fred and appeals to her old
friend Dr. Archie for money with which to go to Germany. Ten years later Thea returns to New York,
having achieved success in Germany and now on the
threshold of a brilliant career with the Metropolitan
Opera. The novel ends with an epilogue set in Moonstone, where Tillie Kronborg, Thea's stage-struck spin-
ster aunt, who had always predicted a brilliant future
for her niece, is vicariously living out the wonder of a
dream come true.

Art had been a symbol of ultimate reality for
Willa Cather since her college years, and the talented
individual's struggle to "make himself born" as an

artist is a direct analogy of mankind's spiritual quest for reality, whatever symbolic form it assumes—truth, art, love. In *The Song of the Lark,* the artist's struggle is a literal one. Thea, returning from her year in Chicago, discovers to her surprise and dismay that even her brothers and sisters "were among the people whom she had always recognized as her natural enemies" (p. 240). The title of Part III, dealing with her second year in Chicago, is "Stupid Faces," representing her enemies in the larger world: everyone from her talented but soulless singing teacher, Bowers, to fashionable sopranos with rich husbands and high opinions of themselves. Despite her contempt of these people, she is spiritually undermined by her contact with them; this is the main source of her unhappiness and frustration, from which she is delivered by her sojourn among the cliff dwellings.

In Panther Canyon the nature of Thea's relationship to the Ancient People and the meaning of her struggle are expressed in symbolic terms. The cliff dwellers, as she recalls later, "taught me the inevitable hardness of human life. No artist gets far who doesn't know that" (p. 463). Thus the artist's quest is identified with the human quest, here expressed in its simplest and most elemental form. Thea is temporarily lifted out of the context of her own literal struggle and is able to see its deeper meanings in her growing awareness of the hard, simple life of the ancient Indians. For them, the physical necessities of life grew organically into symbols of spiritual desire, symbols that endure and are visible to Thea in the empty houses, in the well-beaten path from the cliff houses down to the stream, in the broken fragments of pottery vessels.

Human life, even on its simplest level, is reaching

out toward "something else"; indeed, Willa Cather seemed to be suggesting that there is no truly human life without this reaching out. Thea's quest for "something so far away, so deep, so beautiful . . . that there's nothing one can say about it" (p. 460) has the same origins as the Indians' inarticulate desire that led them to decorate their water vessels. Thea comes to see her endeavor as part of a chain reaching back into the past and binding her to the Ancient People; she is no longer simply an isolated individual struggling to fulfill her personal goals, for she is aware of an obligation to "help to fulfill some desire of the dust that slept there" (p. 306).

Willa Cather is right: after this dramatic and beautifully evocative sequence, the rest of the book is anticlimactic. The further history of Fred Ottenburg— whom Thea does eventually marry—Dr. Archie, and the progress of Thea's career are interesting merely in a reportorial way. Even the heights of artistic transcendence to which Thea attains are described, rather than evoked: a subtle difference, but an important one. Though some of the later accounts of Thea's operatic interpretations are very fine, they remain essentially prose transcriptions of a poetic reality that is pointed to, but never again re-created.

4

Youth and the Bright Medusa

(1920)

The full-length portrait of Thea Kronborg did not exhaust Willa Cather's interest in the artist as a fictional symbol, and she continued to explore it in the short stories published in 1920 (together with four stories from *The Troll Garden*) as *Youth and the Bright Medusa.*

In this collection the image of the world of art and culture as a troll garden, magical but potentially corrupting, is replaced by the equally ambiguous image of the bright Medusa—in mythology a Gorgon, once a beautiful woman, who through the enmity of a goddess was made so hideous that to look upon her face would turn a man to stone. With this image Willa Cather is shifting her emphasis away from the world of art and culture, with its attractions and dangers, and focusing more on the young artist (Perseus, the Gorgon slayer), who is challenging the world (the shining but potentially deadly Medusa).

The first two stories present two genuine artists, Don Hedgers in "Coming, Aphrodite!" and Cressida Garnet in "The Diamond Mine." Both have dealt more or less successfully with the world without compromising their art. They are juxtaposed with two talented individuals who fail to live up to their full artistic promise: in the first story Eden Bower eagerly embraces the temptations of a life of success and glamor; and in the second story Blasius Bouchalka succumbs to the temptations of worldly comfort and ease. In the last two stories, "A Gold Slipper" and "Scandal," the artist Kitty Ayrshire is played against two businessmen, Marshall McKann and Siegmund Stein. The two men have sought the Medusa of worldly success for itself alone and have figuratively and almost literally been turned to stone: McKann is described as having a "pressed-brick-and-cement face" (p. 147),* and Stein, whose name means "stone" in German, is even further committed to a soulless materialism. Stein seems to be transformed into something resembling the horrible Medusa herself—he is "one of the most hideous men in New York" (p. 185). Further, though there is no cause-and-effect relationship between his exploitation of Kitty and the persistent inflammation of the vocal chords which is threatening her career, the juxtaposition of Stein's Medusa-like hideousness and Kitty's loss of her voice—a symbolic freezing of the organ of her art —is suggestive. In the first story the world is a challenge with which, given integrity, the artist can cope; in the last story Kitty's integrity is unmarred, but the encroachments of an increasingly powerful materialistic world threaten her, through no fault of her own.

The downward trend of the stories is paralleled by the passage of time. "Coming, Aphrodite!" takes place in the early 1900s, significantly during the last summer when there were horse-drawn stages on Fifth Avenue. It is just about the turn of the century when, in "The Diamond Mine," Cressida Garnet meets the passionate, fiery Bouchalka, and the story ends with the sinking of the *Titanic* in 1912. The Kitty Ayrshire stories are both set in the present time of their writing, approximately 1916. The world has changed very radically; not only have the horses and hansoms on Fifth Avenue been replaced by automobiles ("mis-shapen and sullen, like an ugly threat in a stream of things that were bright and beautiful and alive" [p. 15]), but World War I has conclusively brought an era of "graceful and gracious human living" (p. 117) to an end.

* Page references in this discussion are to *Youth and the Bright Medusa* (New York: Alfred A. Knopf, 1920).

My Ántonia

(1918)

*M*y *Ántonia,* Willa Cather's best-known novel, is, on the surface, deceptively simple. It seems to be merely what the narrator, Jim Burden, claims in the introduction: all that he can remember of his childhood friend Ántonia Shimerda, a Bohemian girl who embodies for him "the country, the conditions, the whole adventure of [his] childhood." As an evocation of the time of the pioneer and the fleeting "best days" of youth, the novel has been praised for its mellow beauty, but at the same time criticized as a nostalgic and ultimately futile attempt to recapture "the precious, the incommunicable past." But the very enduringness of *My Ántonia,* which testifies to its emotional power, suggests that it is more than a lament for a lost past. Further, the fact that this collection of episodes and vignettes—many of which have nothing to do with Ántonia herself—somehow results in a book of "unified emotional impact"[1] suggests that the novel's seemingly artless surface is actually the result of the most careful artistry.

The key to the structure, I think, lies in Jim's titling his story "*My* Ántonia." Though Ántonia is the center of the novel, her story is mediated through him. She remains the memorable character, but her memorableness derives from what she means to Jim. He, too, provides the key to the symbolic level of the novel. Significantly, we first encounter him on a train, and the story he tells begins with his childhood train journey from his old home in Virginia to his new life on the Nebraska frontier.

The novel thus opens with the motif of the journey, which is most broadly given expression in the pioneer's journey from an old established culture to a raw new land. The literal reality of the pioneer

experience is portrayed through the immigrant Shimerdas; the symbolic meaning of that experience is suggested through Jim's life. His response to the prairie
establishes the frame of reference which gives the pioneer experience its symbolic meaning. Thus, when he
describes the red of the grass giving the prairie "the
colour of wine-stains" (p. 15),* he evokes Homer's
"wine-dark sea." This allusion suggests that Jim's journey is a kind of odyssey; the novel describes his adventures in his journey "home to [him]self" (p. 371),
just as Homer sings of Odysseus's journey home to
Penelope.

Jim deepens further the symbolic meaning of the
prairie glowing in the autumn sunlight when he compares it to the bush that "burned with fire and was not
consumed" (p. 40) out of which the voice of God
spoke to Moses. This image suggests that the prairie
is transparent to the sacred, infused with a tremendous
and awe-inspiring power which cannot be adequately
described but which is testified to in religion and myth.
The sacred, which is "equivalent to a *power,* and, in
the last analysis, to *reality,*" is experienced as "pre-
eminently the *real,* at once power, efficacy, the source
of life and fecundity."[2] Thus the pioneer journey in
general, and Jim's life in particular, become metaphors
for a quest for the power, life, and fecundity which are
manifestations of the sacred, of ultimate reality.

In the presence of the sacred, which is the fullness
of being, man feels his "profound nothingness."[3] Jim's
first reaction to the prairie, as he rides over it at night
to his grandfather's farm, is to feel "erased, blotted

* Page references in this discussion are to *My Ántonia* (Boston: Houghton Mifflin Co., 1918).

out" (p. 8). Though he never uses the words *power* and
reality to characterize this experience of the sacred, Jim
is describing incidents that are clearly charged with
power. Thus, having arrived at the farm, he goes alone
to his grandmother's garden and there surrenders himself completely to a kind of mystic union with being:

I was something that lay under the sun and felt it, like the
pumpkins, and I did not want to be anything more. I was
entirely happy. Perhaps we feel like that when we die and
become a part of something entire, whether it is sun and air,
or goodness and knowledge. At any rate, that is happiness;
to be dissolved into something complete and great. When it
comes to one, it comes as naturally as sleep [p. 18].

The movement of the novel is from this childhood
revelation of the sacred, through the inevitable grow-
ing-away from it as Jim enters adolescence and moves
into the complexities of adult social life as encountered
in the town and the city, to his final rediscovery of the
reality that he had experienced in childhood, now embodied for him in the luminous figure of Ántonia, the
"rich mine of life."

The incidents that flesh out this symbolic life-
journey are utterly realistic and seemingly artless.
Book I is titled "The Shimerdas," and most of it is
focused on Jim Burden's experience with Antonia's
family. The plight of the Shimerdas is intensified by
the implicit contrast with the comfortable, harmonious
family life of the Burdens; ignorant of the language,
cheated by their go-between Krajiek, living like ani-
mals in a dugout that is little better than a cave, they
are, in externals at least, a sorry sight. And the conditions within the family are far from harmonious; the
mother is grasping and mean and has centered all her

ambitions on her surly son Ambrosch. The father, whose major concern is for his beloved Ántonia, is a gentle man of culture and sensitivity, demoralized by his wife and suffering terribly the hardships of prairie life. In the midst of these hardships Ántonia herself, at fourteen, is eager, cheerful, full of life. Without ever ceasing to be her exuberant, particular self, she is already beginning to become, for Jim, the personification of life itself.

Christmas comes, and with it a visit by Mr. Shimerda to the Burdens to thank them for their kindness to his family. Mr. Shimerda has already promised Jim his fine gun when the boy is grown, suggesting that he regards Jim in some way as a spiritual heir. When Mr. Shimerda looks at him, Jim feels "as if he were looking far ahead into the future for me, down the road I would have to travel" (p. 87). As he leaves, the old man blesses Jim with the sign of the cross. This scene suggests the blessing of a biblical patriarch given to his chosen son and emphasizes the symbolic spiritual relationship between Mr. Shimerda and Jim. In January news comes that Mr. Shimerda has killed himself. Though Jim's account of the story of the suicide and the burial is laconic and unemotional, the episode is one of deep importance to him, as is suggested in his later reflection on Mr. Shimerda's grave: "I never came upon the place without emotion, and in all that country it was the spot most dear to me" (p. 119).

Book I ends in midsummer, with the completion of the cycle of the year which began with Jim's and the Shimerdas' arrival on the prairie. Book II, "The Hired Girls," opens three years later in the town of Black Hawk, where Jim's grandparents have moved. The prairie experience gives way to the town experi-

ence for Ántonia as well when Jim's grandmother
arranges for her to come to work as a hired girl for
their next-door neighbors, the Harlings.

Life on the prairie was hard physically, but life
in town is hard in more subtle ways. Though the town
offers the pleasures of social life, Jim soon becomes
aware of the class distinctions that are a part of town
consciousness. The young men of Black Hawk's American families—including Jim—are naturally drawn to
the vigor and attractiveness of immigrants' daughters
like Ántonia and the pretty Norwegian Lena Lingard.
But the social consciousness of the town has decreed
that Black Hawk boys should marry Black Hawk girls,
which, after some longing glances at the hired girls,
they do. When a dancing pavilion opens, however, the
town boys and the country girls can meet on neutral
ground, and the girls are seen more than ever as a
"menace to the social order" (p. 201). For Ántonia the
dancing pavilion becomes irresistible, and her success
there brings a stream of admirers to the Harlings' back
door. When Mr. Harling objects, Ántonia leaves his
household rather than give up her dancing and goes
to work for Wick Cutter, a moneylender with an evil
reputation. The fullness of life that Ántonia embodies
is thus symbolically cast out of the homes of respectable
families, and Ántonia herself is exposed to attempted
rape by the unsavory Cutter and, finally, to seduction
and abandonment by the handsome ne'er-do-well Larry
Donovan.

Jim senses the "evasions and negations" of life in
the homes of Black Hawk's American families, where
"every individual taste, every natural appetite, was
bridled by caution" (p. 219). But socially he "belongs"
in those houses, not in the Bohemian saloon where he

likes to drop in and listen to the immigrants talk, and not at the Firemen's Hall where, at Saturday night dances, he meets the hired girls and others who used to come to the dancing pavilion. He seeks the exuberance of life at the dances, but there are dangers there as well: the soft, sensual danger of Lena Lingard, against whom Ántonia warns him. She senses that Jim's life must be a quest—"to make something of yourself," as she puts it—from which Lena will distract him.

The quest as symbol is given its most specific form at Jim's country picnic with Ántonia and her friends. Ántonia asks Jim to tell them of the story of Coronado and his search for the Seven Golden Cities. Though the history books say that Coronado had not reached Nebraska, Jim is convinced that he had been along the very river where he and the girls are now sitting; not far north of there a farmer had dug up a metal stirrup of fine workmanship and a sword with the name of a Spanish maker. The girls ask unanswerable questions about Coronado's quest, but Jim can only tell them what the schoolbooks say: that he " 'died in the wilderness, of a broken heart.' " Symbolically identifying her father's quest with Coronado's, Ántonia murmurs sadly, " 'More than him has done that' " (p. 244). Caught up in the mood of the moment, Jim and the girls watch the sun go down.

The link between Mr. Shimerda and Coronado is made explicit as a gigantic black image of a plow, magnified by the horizontal light, leaps up against the setting disc of the sun. The plow is the symbol of the pioneer on the plains. Coronado and Mr. Shimerda were spiritual pioneers, just as the families of the hired girls, which have endured such rigors and discomforts on the wild prairie, are pioneers in the physical sense.

It is the mark that the pioneer spirit has left on them that makes the hired girls superior to the Black Hawk girls. The hired girls are, in their different ways and degrees, the embodiment of life in its generosity and abundance. Jim recognizes this more clearly when the realization comes to him that "if there were no girls like them in the world, there would be no poetry" (p. 270), for poetry is born out of man's awareness of a depth of reality underneath seemingly commonplace things. Here is suggested one aspect of Jim's quest. He has no professional ambition to be an artist, but on the deeper levels of his life he will encounter the task of poetry: to recreate, in his account of Ántonia, the reality that she embodies for him.

Not long afterward, Jim goes off to the university at Lincoln. His first year there is a time of great mental excitement as his narrow horizons are opened to the classical past. In his sophomore year, however, Lena Lingard seeks him out. She is now established as a dressmaker in Lincoln and is well on her way to becoming a business success. But she is still the same lazy, innocently voluptuous Lena, offering a kind of opium dream of sensuality, promising endless pleasure, but leading nowhere. Dallying with her, Jim loses interest in his classes and drifts aimlessly until his academic mentor urges him to break with Lena and follow him to Harvard. Before leaving for the east, Jim visits his grandparents' farm, where he learns from the tenant of Ántonia's betrayal by Larry Donovan. Ántonia had gone to Denver expecting to be married to Donovan there, but she had returned sadly a few months later saying that Donovan had deserted her after her money gave out and had not married her. Ántonia then went to live on her brother Ambrosch's farm, where she gave birth to her illegitimate baby.

When Jim goes to visit Ántonia the next day they instinctively walk toward Mr. Shimerda's grave as "the fittest place to talk to each other" (p. 319). Here, in the presence of her father, Ántonia and Jim affirm that the relationship between them is not dependent on their physical proximity. Jim realizes that Ántonia is symbolically the center of his life: "'I'd have liked to have you for a sweetheart, or a wife, or my mother or my sister—anything that a woman can be to a man'" (p. 321). Anything that woman, as the spiritual counterpart of man, can be, Ántonia is to Jim. He holds a comparable position in her life, and she will immortalize him in the stories she will tell of him to her children, just as he will immortalize her in writing *My Ántonia*.

Jim says little about the next twenty years which elapse before he visits Ántonia again, but we can deduce that they have not been easy. He confesses that he has put off going to see Ántonia for fear of having his image of her shattered by reality, as apparently has happened to many other of what he calls his "illusions." We know from the introduction that he has a childless and rather unsympathetic wife and has suffered unspecified "disappointments." Though on the surface his life seems spiritually barren, in his work as a railroad lawyer he has given expression to his deep love for the country through which his railway runs, and "his faith in it and his knowledge of it have played an important part in its development." He visits Ántonia not expecting anything, only to find that all he thought he had left behind is given to him again.

Ántonia he finds "battered but not diminished" (p. 332). She is surrounded by a dozen loving and lively children, who show Jim the new cave for storing preserves and then come pouring out of the darkness of the cave like "a veritable explosion of life" (p. 339). Reflecting on the pictures of Ántonia in his memory, Jim concludes that he was not mistaken, they are not illusions: "She was a battered woman now, not a lovely girl; but she still had that something which fires the imagination, could still stop one's breath for a moment by a look or gesture that somehow revealed the meaning in common things" (p. 353).

This image of Ántonia is so clear and so evocative that it scarcely needs comment. In her ability to give herself so completely to the task of life, she at once fulfills her individual nature and transcends it; without ceasing to be Ántonia, without even realizing what she is doing, she lends herself "to immemorial human attitudes which we recognize by instinct as universal and true." She seems to embody, in her everyday life, that self-surrender Jim experienced as a boy when he lay in his grandmother's sun-warmed garden and experienced the happiness of being dissolved into something complete and great. Her life does not merely extend in the horizontal dimension from birth to death, but descends vertically into the depths of life, into the realm of the imagintaion and the spirit. As she lives in this dimension of depth her life makes this dimension present for others; it is that quality in her that "fires the imagination" and that illuminates her simplest actions and charges them with transcendent meaning.

For Jim, Ántonia is the gateway back to his childhood, when he too experienced the vertical dimension of life. Thus, as he wanders over the traces of the old road on which he was driven to his grandparents' farm that first night many years ago, he has the "sense of coming home to myself, and of [finding] out what a little circle man's experience is" (pp. 371–72). It is, of course, a literal homecoming and completing of the circle, back to the very road with which the novel began, and ending as it began in the autumn of the year. But more important is Jim's sense of returning to an awareness of the deep sources of his life, as symbolized in his childhood, in the land, and in Ántonia.

of 166. This is a reduced representation of the original page.

6

One of Ours
(1922)

In May of 1918 Willa Cather learned of the death in World War I of her young cousin, G. P. Cather, Jr., a Nebraska boy of whom she had been very fond. When the boy's mother gave her his letters to read, Willa Cather found in them the story of an uncertain young man's discovery of himself and the world of values through his wartime experience. This became the theme of her next novel, *One of Ours*. In the situations surrounding her cousin's life and his death, she saw a paradigm of what she felt was happening in American life: the pioneer spirit, as symbolized in the breaking of the plains, the fecundation of American culture through the transplantation of immigrant stock to American soil, had been superseded by a new era in which prosperity had produced a life that was materially easier, but spiritually more and more barren.

Claude Wheeler, the fictional character modeled on G. P. Cather, Jr., finds none of the resources in his life that were available to the earlier generation. He is strong and gifted with a generous, idealistic nature—the characteristics of Willa Cather's true pioneers—but his modern environment has no understanding of those gifts and laughs at him for his inability to "get on." As a result, Claude's strength is turned against himself. As a social being he cannot escape the compelling pressure of his environment, and he exhausts himself trying to subdue his nature so that he can live like everyone else.

There is a tremendous potential of pathos in the story of Claude's efforts to adjust himself to life around him. But this pathos is unfortunately never realized because of the reportorial style of the book. Claude's situation and his environment are reported in detail and with great credibility, but with few exceptions

(Mahailey, the simple-minded servant is one) the people who comprise Claude's world are described rather than evoked. We observe Claude's suffering but we do not suffer with him. As a result we fail to perceive the legitimacy and depth of his suffering. Willa Cather perhaps thought this was necessary to convey a sense of the emotional dryness of the world in which Claude lived; but unfortunately it greatly reduces the novel's potential impact.

Artistically, *One of Ours* is one of Willa Cather's least successful novels, but in terms of content and themes it is more significant than is usually recognized. It is very carefully constructed, with every major character representing a way of life or a point of view. Claude's father is a hard, jocular man who has the pioneer's energy and force but who turns that strength toward a variety of activities of no enduring value. Even his potentially finest quality—his vast enjoyment of life—is expressed in sometimes cruel harassment of what he considers weakness and false pride in his wife and in Claude. Claude's elder brother, Bayliss, is an undersized young man with a mean, dyspeptic temperament and a penchant for making money. While his father is a morally neutral figure whose abundant energy is given no meaningful direction, Bayliss possesses a narrow stream of energy consciously directed at purely selfish and materialistic ends. Claude's mother, a former schoolteacher and a woman of some culture, is gentle and sensitive but weak. A pious woman, she has made her adjustment to life by clinging to a faith represented by "smooth-talking preachers," and can only hope that Claude will "find his Saviour" and thereby cease finding life so difficult.

There is one person in Claude's farm environment

who has something of his own vitality and sensibility, the schoolteacher and musician, Gladys Farmer. The generosity and fullness of her nature are expressed in what the townsfolk criticize as her extravagance. Though barely able to support herself and her mother on her salary, she is willing to spend what little she has for things of beauty. But she seems to be accepting the attentions of Bayliss, and Claude turns away from her bitterly disappointed, thinking that she is willing to pocket her fine feelings in exchange for the security of being a rich man's wife.

Thus cut off from Gladys, Claude is thrown together, through a series of unfortunate circumstances, with Enid Royce. While he is convalescent after an accident she faithfully visits him, and he falls in love with her. Enid, like Claude's mother, is devoutly religious; she longed to be a missionary in China, as her sister is, but failing that she is a local worker for the cause of prohibition. Claude hopes for great things in his marriage with Enid, believing it will miraculously change this "cool, self-satisfied girl into a loving and generous one" (p. 177).* But the marriage is a disaster, and Claude, who had looked forward to be "wonderfully happy in love" (p. 210), suffers deeply and confusedly.

Claude senses the captive spirit languishing inside himself and others, especially his mother, Mahailey, and Gladys, feeling them to be "people whose hearts were set high . . . whose wish was so beautiful that there were no experiences in this world to satisfy it" (p. 207). Gladys, too, has intimations of this sort:

* Page references in this discussion are to *One of Ours* (New York: Alfred A. Knopf, 1922).

She believed that all things which might make the world beautiful—love and kindness, leisure and art—were shut up in prison, and that successful men like Bayliss Wheeler held the keys. The generous ones, who would let these things out to make people happy, were somehow weak, and could not break the bars. . . . There were people, even in Frankfort, who had imagination and generous impulses, but they were all, she had to admit, inefficient—failures [p. 155].

Gladys's one hope has been that Claude will succeed, will break out of those confining bars; but she fears that, married to Enid, he "would become one of those dead people that moved about the streets of Frankfort; everything that was Claude would perish, and the shell of him would come and go and eat and sleep for fifty years" (p. 154–55). Claude is saved from the fulfillment of Gladys's prediction by Enid's sister falling seriously ill in China and by the war in Europe. Enid feels it her duty to leave Claude and go to her sister; a few months later, in April of 1917, the United States declares war on Germany, and Claude enlists in the army.

Most of the negative criticism which *One of Ours* received was directed toward the section set in France during the last years of the war. Many critics found the war scenes unconvincing and objected to what they felt was Willa Cather's "sentimentalization" of the war. Though the second half of the novel is romantic in tone and feeling, Willa Cather makes it perfectly clear that she has no illusions about the war making "the world safe for Democracy, or any rhetoric of that sort" (p. 409). As far as the novel is concerned, she is not dealing with the war as a political event, nor is she treating it on a realistic level.

A comparison of the structure of *One of Ours* with

The Song of the Lark illuminates the function of the section set in wartime France. In both novels the central character needs to escape from the confining ways of small-town thinking, and in both this is accomplished through a sojourn in another country rich in ancient traditions. For Thea, the cliff dwellings are a way station which make it possible for her to continue her quest for artistic fulfillment; for Claude, France is the journey's end. Willa Cather's use of the same device in the earlier novel makes it clear that in this novel France is a symbolic landscape and the war primarily an instrument for providing the stark contrast of death against which the essential reality of life can be most sharply revealed.

The transition between the rather flat realism of the Nebraska scenes and the increasingly romantic tone of those in France is made gradually; small vignettes appear in the narrative that for the first time have a quality of depth, that reach beyond the immediate present and suggest deeper and more enduring realities. In one such incident, Claude simply sits for an hour in the church of Saint Ouen while the light from the rose window streams over him. He compares this light to light from a star which traveled through space for hundreds of years before it got to him. The light is like an avenue through time and space going through him and beyond him, linking him and his short personal past with the depth of the French past, intersecting his horizontal path with the vertical dimension. There is also an implicit contrast between Claude's experience of beauty and depth in the French church and his experience at home with the religion of Enid and her preacher, Brother Weldon; the one, Claude instinctively recognizes, is palpably real, the other embarrassingly false.

As Claude comes in closer contact with the reality of death he is given, through the fortunes of war, an experience which reveals to him more of the essential meaning of life. After his first days in the trenches he is sent on an errand that enables him to make a visit to a devastated town. Though the town has been reduced to rubble, the old inhabitants have been coming back, and a Red Cross barrack, with emergency foodstuffs and supplies, has been set up in a ruined convent garden on the top of a hill. Claude makes his way there, and meets Mademoiselle de Courcy. The care lavished on the ruined garden and on the simple interior of the barracks is one visible aspect of a pervasive mood of wholeness and clarity that the scene evokes. Mademoiselle de Courcy articulates what Claude has been sensing: "This war has taught us all how little the made things matter. Only the feeling matters" (p. 386). Again, there is an implicit contrast with the superficial quality of life in Claude's Nebraska environment, where value is placed on "made things" and men work the land for money and without love.

Claude's encounters with French life between military engagements are charged with quiet but deep meaning: his return, after a brush with death, to the household of the Jouberts, where he is billeted and where he is met with genuine affection; his visit to the nearby woods, which are described with lambent beauty and which evoke a sense of ancient peace, of the quiet depths of life flowing on beneath the surface violence of the war. With his co-officer David Gerhardt, a former violinist who represents to Claude all that is admirable and worthy of emulation, he visits the home of a French family of the *haute bourgeoisie*. He is torn between admiration and bitter envy, feeling himself awkward and undeveloped among people who have a heritage of beauty, culture, and discipline. Out of this encounter Claude comes to the realization that he had never known that "there was anything worth living for, till this war came on. Before that, the world seemed like a business proposition." A "business proposition," however dull, may seem more harmless than the enormous physical and mental cruelties of war, but Claude is responding out of a radical awareness that it profits a man nothing to gain the whole world and lose his soul, and that to live in a soulless world, as he knows from his own experience, is to be in danger of a worse death than any death in war.

No battlefield or shattered country he had seen was as ugly as this world would be if men like his brother Bayliss controlled it altogether. Until the war broke out, he had supposed they did control it; his boyhood had been clouded and enervated by that belief. The Prussians had believed it, too, apparently. But the event had shown that there were a great many people left who cared about something else [p. 419].

The very fact that there is a war is proof to Claude that men like his brother Bayliss will not prevail; the very sound of the guns tells him

that men could still die for an idea; and would burn all they had made to keep their dreams. He knew the future of the world was safe; the careful planners would never be able to put it into a straight-jacket,—cunning and prudence would never have it to themselves. . . . Ideals were not archaic

things, beautiful and impotent; they were the real sources
of power among men. As long as that was true, and now he
knew it was true—he had come all this way to find out—he
had no quarrel with Destiny [pp. 419–20].

Significantly, Claude's final test is a choice between
prudence and idealism: to let his men, confused and
demoralized by an explosion that has blown up their
gun emplacements, flee from the advancing enemy, or
to hold them in their position and try to check the
enemy onslaught. He springs up to the parapet of the
trench to direct their fire and senses that the confusion
of the men is falling away as they respond to his leader-
ship: "he had his men in hand. . . . With these men
he could do anything. He had learned the mastery of
men" (p. 452). It is his most exalted moment. He holds
the line for the twenty minutes needed for the re-
inforcements to be brought up, and falls mortally
wounded as they appear.

Up to this point, the novel, whatever its weaknesses, has been relatively simple: for the man of feeling, dying for an ideal is preferable to living without
one. After Claude's death, however, Willa Cather raises
the disquieting question of whether idealism can, after
all, survive in the modern world. Rereading his letters,
Claude's mother muses that he "died believing his own
country better than it is, and France better than any
country can ever be. And those were beautiful beliefs
to die with. Perhaps it was as well to see that vision,
and then to see no more" (p. 458). Claude's mother
speaks out of the deepest pity and sympathy for her
son and finds comfort in the fact that death spared him
the terrible disillusion that drove to suicide other
heroes who survived the war. Her sentiments imply,
however, that there is, indeed, no place in the world

for extravagant hope and passionate belief, that such hopes and beliefs, however inspiring and beautiful, are ultimately illusory. They may enable one to die meaningfully, but they do not enable one to live.

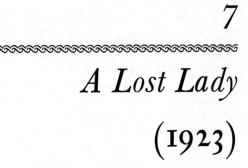

7

A Lost Lady

(1923)

When *A Lost Lady* appeared in 1923 it was immediately acclaimed as a "nearly perfect" novel.[1] A brief, beautifully evocative portrait, it puts into practice the theory of fiction Willa Cather sketched in her 1922 essay "The Novel Démeublé" ("unfurnished"), in which she deplored the use of a great deal of materialistic detail in serious imaginative writing. "The higher processes of art," she wrote, "are all processes of simplification."[2] The artist does not create a sense of reality by enumerating all the physical details of a scene, but rather by selecting those very few necessary things that will convey an emotional aura and a reality of feeling that the reader experiences without being told about. Though the scenes of *A Lost Lady* are filled with warm descriptive detail, there is nothing extraneous, nothing that does not contribute to the total effect of the novel.

The story is simple. It came to Willa Cather in 1921 when she received news of the death of the wife of Nebraska's former governor Silas Garber, one of the founders of Red Cloud. The big Garber house with its grove of cottonwood trees was dear to Willa Cather, and in her childhood she had extravagantly admired the governor's beautiful and charming young wife. Governor Garber's loss of his money, his stroke, his death, the departure of his widow and her eventual remarriage provided the outline of the story. In the novel Mrs. Garber becomes Marian Forrester, the young wife of Captain Daniel Forrester, a builder of railroads and a leading citizen in the prairie town of Sweet Water. The story is presented through a series of significant episodes, which are seen largely through the eyes of young Niel Herbert, to whom Mrs. Forrester is the embodiment of beauty and graciousness.

As a boy of twelve, picnicking in the Forrester's grove, Niel breaks his arm falling out of a tree in an attempt to rescue a bird that an older boy, Ivy Peters, has cruelly blinded. Carried into Mrs. Forrester's bedroom to await the arrival of the doctor, Niel absorbs the quiet elegance of the room and thinks that "he would probably never be in so nice a place again" (p. 28).*

In addition to evoking Mrs. Forrester's winning charm and the beauty of the Forrester house and land, this initial episode suggests the assumptions that underlie the Forresters' life. Mrs. Forrester is friendly to all of the boys, but she is aware of the social distinctions between Niel, who is the nephew of her husband's friend Judge Pommeroy, and the "town boys," sons of local grocers and tailors. The boys themselves recognize that she is "a very special kind of person" and feel that the privileged class to which she belongs is "an axiomatic fact in the social order" (p. 19). Their admiration and instinctive respect for her is contrasted to the insolence of Ivy Peters—insolence that Mrs. Forrester deals with courteously but firmly. As Ivy's moral and physical ugliness is antagonistic to the wildlife and to the physical beauty of the Forrester grove, his presence also suggests a threat to the social equilibrium that the other boys accept and take for granted.

The next episodes take place some seven years later. Captain Forrester has had an accident which has brought his career as a railroad builder to an end, and the prospects of the town of Sweet Water have faded because of heavy crop failures. Niel, now nineteen and reading law in Judge Pommeroy's office, is included in

* Page references in this discussion are to *A Lost Lady* (New York: Alfred A. Knopf, 1923).

his uncle's social visits to the Forresters'. There he meets the handsome, powerful Frank Ellinger, whose presence is magnetic but in whom Niel senses something evil. Mrs. Forrester, who thrives on excitement and attention, suffers severely from the dullness of a winter in Sweet Water and begins to drink too much.

Early the next summer Captain Forrester is called suddenly to Denver because of a bank failure, and a few days later Frank Ellinger arrives in town. Awakened early one morning, Niel is overcome with a desire to watch the summer dawn flame up over the Forrester marsh. The glorious freshness of the morning intoxicates him, and he picks a bunch of wild roses to leave outside the French windows of Mrs. Forrester's bedroom. Just as he is placing the flowers on the sill he hears from inside a woman's laughter, and then another laugh, a man's. Blinded with anger and dismay, Niel flees and throws the roses into a mudhole. He feels that he has lost "one of the most beautiful things in his life. . . . It was not a moral scruple she had outraged, but an aesthetic ideal" (pp. 86–87).

By the time the Captain returns from Denver, he has been ruined financially; in order to protect the savings of the workingmen depositors, he has met the bank's losses out of his personal resources. Mrs. Forrester accepts his action proudly and bravely, though it will be hard for her to live in pinched financial circumstances. Immediately after this, Captain Forrester suffers a stroke; he recovers, but he drags his left foot, and his speech is thick.

Part II opens with Niel's return to Sweet Water after two years at college. The first person he meets is Ivy Peters, now a shyster lawyer, who tells him that he has rented and drained the Forrester marsh and planted it in wheat. Niel feels that Ivy drained the marsh "quite as much to spite him and Mrs. Forrester as to reclaim the land" (p. 105). The old world, with its beauty and graciousness and order, suggested by the opening pages of Part I, is past and is being supplanted by a new age of men like Ivy Peters—mean-souled, materialistic, destructive of beauty. Ivy makes it his business to be at the Forrester place frequently and treats Mrs. Forrester in a presumptuous and familiar way. When Niel takes her to task for putting up with Ivy, she replies with real anxiety that they simply have to get along with him; she is referring to their financial dependence on his rent and on some questionable investments he has made for her. But she also seems instinctively to realize that Ivy represents the direction in which the world is going, to which she believes she must accommodate herself in order to survive.

When the Captain suffers another stroke, Mrs. Forrester goes completely to pieces. She loses her old ability to keep people courteously in their place; her house is overrun by the malignantly curious and gossipy townswomen who come on the pretext of bringing soups for the invalid and leave to discuss Mrs. Forrester's state and the condition of her linens. Niel decides to stay out of school for a year and take care of the Forresters. He drives away the gossips and takes a deep satisfaction in bringing quiet back to the house again; when the Forresters are sleeping he keeps vigil with "the old things that had seemed so beautiful to him in his childhood" (p. 142).

Captain Forrester dies in December, and shortly afterward Mrs. Forrester transfers her legal affairs from Judge Pommeroy to Ivy Peters, who is more and more in evidence at the Forrester house. Niel finds that Mrs.

Forrester, far from being freed of a burden by the
death of her husband and thus enabled to be her former, lighthearted, charming self, has changed for the
worse; she is flighty and perverse, "like a ship without
ballast, driven hither and thither by every wind" (p.
152). Niel is bitterly disappointed at the change in her,
and when he happens to see Ivy casually embracing her
in her kitchen, he is filled with such disgust that he
goes back to college without even bidding her goodbye.
He reflects that all those years

> he had thought it was Mrs. Forrester who made that house
> so different from any other. But ever since the Captain's
> death it was a house where old friends, like his uncle, were
> betrayed and cast off, where common fellows behaved after
> their kind and knew a common woman when they saw her
> [p. 170].

Some years later Niel hears that Mrs. Forrester has
at last sold her house and left Sweet Water. With the
passage of time he forgets his chagrin and remembers
her as she had been in her best days, when her eyes
seemed to promise something no one else had ever
found. He wonders

> whether she had really found some ever-blooming, ever-
> burning, ever-piercing joy, or whether it was all fine play-
> acting. Probably she had found no more than another; but
> she had always the power of suggesting things much lovelier
> than herself, as the perfume of a single flower may call up
> the whole sweetness of spring [p. 172].

Niel hears once more of his "long-lost lady" when a
boyhood friend tells him that he met her by chance in
South America; she had married a rich old Englishman
who, though reputedly stingy, treated her well and

provided her with the kind of life she needed as long as she lived.

A Lost Lady is similar to *My Ántonia* in that the heroine is presented primarily in terms of what she means to a boy or young man through whose eyes her life is seen. Thus, *A Lost Lady* is not simply the story of the moral decline of a fascinating and mysteriously attractive woman; it has another dimension in Niel's experience of her story and in what it embodies for him. This dimension is seen most clearly in the life of Captain Forrester. Though Mrs. Forrester occupies the center of the stage, it is against the background of his life that she takes on her symbolic meaning.

Captain Forrester was one of the great pioneers of railroad building in the west, one of a group of men whom Willa Cather depicts as visionary, idealistic, innately noble. To these men the tremendous goal of putting "plains and mountains under the iron harness" (p. 168) was an achievement as much spiritual as physical, one that involved men's awareness of their relationship to the plains and mountains and was not an exploitation or desecration of them. Springing out of Captain Forrester's well-grounded physical and moral strength is an aesthetic sensibility which manifests itself in his love of natural beauty—his selection of the site of his house, long before the town of Sweet Water even existed, because the hilltop "looked beautiful to him" (p. 11); his leaving his marshy meadows an uncultivated refuge for wildfowl rather than draining the land and making it productive; his care, in his retirement, for his roses and his garden; and most of all, his choice of, and delight in, his beautiful wife.

In his strength, his integrity, and his appreciation of beauty, Captain Forrester is a symbolic representa-

tive of the flowering of life in the pioneer era. Those
first settlers were "dreamers, great-hearted adventurers
who were unpractical to the point of magnificence"
(p. 106); a generous, courteous brotherhood that built
a society that reflected their fine qualities in its graciousness and ease. The financial success which makes
this society possible is to some extent taken for granted,
but never sought as an end in itself. Captain Forrester,
indeed, virtually pauperizes himself after the bank
failure in order to make good the accounts of the depositors. The material comforts of his life may be
dependent on wealth, but the spiritual core that in-
fuses those comforts and gives them harmony and
meaning is not. No amount of money can ennoble a
man like Frank Ellinger, much less Ivy Peters. The pioneer era that Captain Forrester represents is first of all
a condition of the spirit.

   The decline of that era is symbolized in two
primary ways: in the physical decline of Captain Forrester, and in the presence of younger men who sup-
plant him. Frank Ellinger is only half a generation
younger than the Captain, but he represents the al-
ready-present decline from pioneer standards. The contrast between the two men is illustrated by vignettes
of their youth: while Captain Forrester worked hard
driving supply wagons across the unbroken plains from
Nebraska to Denver, Frank Ellinger was a fast young
dandy who squired the madam of a Denver brothel
about the city in his carriage in broad daylight. Ivy
Peters, a full generation younger than the Captain, is
a representative of the coming man of the modern era
who covets power and wealth and who is opposed to
all of the values and beauty intrinsic in the Forresters'
life. While Ellinger still has the attractiveness and

forcefulness of the pioneer, though admixed with coarseness, Ivy Peters is unredeemably ugly, with hard little eyes like a snake and an instinctive animosity toward life.

Symbolically, Marian Forrester is beauty, charm, vitality, the fit ornament to crown her husband's life and reflect, in aesthetic terms, the solid values that are at its base. Even though Niel virtually idolized her, he recognizes that

it was in relation to her husband that he most admired her. Given her other charming attributes, her comprehension of a man like the railroad-builder, her loyalty to him, stamped her more than anything else. That, he felt, was quality. . . . His admiration of Mrs. Forrester went back to that, just as, he felt, she herself went back to it [p. 78].

This is an extremely significant perception; as long as Mrs. Forrester is rooted in her husband's life, she is transfused, as it were, with his values, and she is capable of nobility and even self-sacrifice. But her husband's physical and financial decline is accompanied by increasing signs of moral decline in her. She is without inner resources of her own, and as her husband's symbolic power becomes diminished she gravitates first into a passionate infatuation with Ellinger and later into a kind of political accommodation with Ivy Peters.

The first relationship, however coarsening it is to her—leading to her half-drunken, angry recriminations to Ellinger when she learns of his marriage—is not an unusual occurrence when a beautiful woman is married to an older and physically incapacitated man. Captain Forrester himself is aware of the relationship and seems to tolerate it with compassionate understanding.

But the relationship with Ivy Peters is motivated by fear and self-interest, and Mrs. Forrester becomes, underneath her beautiful surface, a grasping, unprincipled woman who shows neither discretion nor good sense. Such integrity as she had was rooted in her husband; without him she has only her aesthetic qualities, which she bravely and rather pathetically marshals for Ivy Peters and the town boys, like a great old actress reduced to doing scenes from her past triumphs to a vaudeville audience.

But as *A Lost Lady* is not merely an evocative portrait of Marian Forrester, neither is it merely a nostalgic tribute to the greatness of the pioneers. Willa Cather uses the pioneer era as a symbol or an extended metaphor, not as a literal depiction of reality. As with the figure of Mrs. Forrester, it is the pioneer era as it appears to Niel, who had come upon it "when its glory was nearly spent," as a traveler might come upon a buffalo hunter's fire after the hunter was gone: "the coals would be trampled out, but the ground was warm, and the flattened grass where he had slept and where his pony had grazed, told the story" (p. 168). The story that it tells is the stuff of heroic legend, not history. This even Mrs. Forrester unconsciously recognizes as she begins her story of how she met and married the Captain "once upon a time."

8

The Professor's House

(1925)

On the flyleaf of Robert Frost's copy of *The Professor's House,* Willa Cather wrote that the novel was about "letting go with the heart"—a reference to Frost's poem "Wild Grapes."[1] The protagonist in the poem concludes that she has learned to let go with the hands and the mind but not with the heart, and has, indeed, no wish or need to do so. Professor Godfrey St. Peter, Willa Cather's protagonist, has to learn to let go with the heart as well. The rigorousness of this conclusion, which Willa Cather does not soften in the least, makes *The Professor's House* more problematical than any of her earlier works. Even more than in *A Lost Lady,* Willa Cather withholds authorial comment. We see St. Peter as he is undergoing a critical period in his life, before he has begun to understand it or reflect upon it. As a result, we come close to the experience of going through it with him, with all the ambiguity, uncertainty, and contradictoriness involved in a struggle through a crisis that is painfully suffered but not yet understood.

A professor of history at a midwestern state university, St. Peter has recently completed his life work, an eight-volume history of the Spanish adventurers in North America, which has won the Oxford prize. In addition to academic recognition, the prize has brought him five thousand pounds, with which his wife, Lillian, has built a new house. The symbolic core of the novel is the professor's "house" or, actually, houses: the old rented house in which he has spent all his married life and written his great work; and the new house into which, as the novel opens, he is just moving. Though the old house is ugly and inconvenient, with stairs too steep and halls too cramped, St. Peter is reluctant to leave it. He has, in fact, refused to move out of his cramped third-floor workroom, which he has shared with Augusta, the German Catholic sewing woman. When Augusta comes to move her sewing things, St. Peter refuses to let her take the dress forms, insisting that he cannot have the room changed if he is going to work in it. These forms—a bust and a wire-skirted figure—introduce a symbolic comment on St. Peter's domestic life: though he wants them because of their pleasant associations with his daughters' girlhood, their description is clearly indicative of deceptive comfort and heartless femininity.

Part of St. Peter's affection for his old house stems from the "engaging drama of domestic life" which went on beneath his workroom. But even more important to him is the creative work that went on in the attic room—the symbolic "mind" of the house—fed by the warmth of the domestic heart below. Thus, his happy memories of his daughters' childhood are intertwined with his memories of those same years as the years in which "he was beginning to do his great work . . . years when he had the courage to say to himself: 'I will do this dazzling, this beautiful, this utterly impossible thing!' " (p. 25).* But the very success of his work has put "those golden days" irrevocably behind him and has, literally as well as figuratively, brought him "the new house into which he did not want to move" (p. 33).

This new house reflects the St. Peters' increased social status and Lillian's increasingly materialistic ambitions. Associated with this house is the new way of life that St. Peter's family has developed since the

---

* Page references in this discussion are to *The Professor's House* (New York: Alfred A. Knopf, 1925).

marriage of his daughter Rosamund to Louie Marsellus, a gregarious, exuberant, and charming Jew. An
electrical engineer, Louie has quickly become wealthy
through his commercial development of a scientific
discovery made by Rosamund's former fiancé, Tom
Outland. Tom, who was killed in World War I, had
willed the rights to the invention to Rosamund. Mrs.
St. Peter clearly enjoys her son-in-law's social and financial success, his worldliness and sophistication, his
frank joy in acquiring just the right accoutrements
for his new country house or just the right clothes
and jewels for his beautiful wife. But Louie and his
money have inadvertently poisoned the relationships
within the family. Kathleen, Rosamund's once-adoring
younger sister, cannot forgive Rosamund for forget-
ting Tom Outland and marrying Louie; and Louie's
money and his adulation of Rosamund's beauty have
made Rosamund proud and scornful. She is arrogant
and subtly hateful toward Kathleen, and Kathleen is
devoured with resentment and envy of her. Kathleen's
husband, Scott, who was Tom Outland's friend, is resentful and jealous that Louie, who never knew Tom,
seems to have appropriated Tom for himself.

In the new house, the house of success, St. Peter is
increasingly uncomfortable. " 'All is vanity!' " (p. 49) he
says lightly to his wife, and the new house is indeed
imbued with enough petty ambitions to cause St. Peter
to reflect, like the writer of Ecclesiastes, upon the ultimate meaninglessness of human enterprises. All of
Tom Outland's youthful idealism, the magical "desire"
that burned in him, which St. Peter so reverenced and
which fed both Tom's discovery of some cliff dwellings
and his scientific work, has been lost to those who have
profited by Tom's "success." St. Peter wonders, with

some pain, what would have happened to Tom himself had he lived to have the "trap of worldly success" (p. 260) sprung on him:

He couldn't see Tom building "Outland" [the name given by the Marselluses to their pretentious country house], or becoming a public-spirited citizen of Hamilton. What change would have come in his blue eye, in his fine long hand . . . which had never handled things that were not the symbols of ideas? A hand like that, had he lived, must have been put to other uses. His fellow scientists, his wife, the town and State, would have required many duties of it. It would have had to write thousands of useless letters, frame thousands of false excuses. It would have had to "manage" a great deal of money, to be the instrument of a woman who would grow always more and more exacting. He had escaped all that. He had made something new in the world—and the rewards, the meaningless conventional gestures, he had left to others [pp. 260–61].

The "desire" that manifests itself in creation, that St. Peter specifically identifies with creation, is of a different and higher order of experience.

Both Tom and St. Peter had "made something new in the world," the one a discovery in physics, the other an original work of scholarship. Both had made achievements that are essentially artistic and, for that reason alone, in addition to whatever utilitarian worth they might have, are of value to the human community. But worldly success, at best, is incommensurate with the joys of creation—St. Peter would gladly pay back his prize money if he could have again the fun he had writing his history—and, at worst, is destructive to the very spirit that led to creation.

St. Peter, having thus before him the picture of the successful life as embodied by his family, is captured

for the reader at this critical moment of choice: to ac-
cede to the kind of life that is expected of him, to enjoy
the worldly rewards of his creative endeavor, or to
deny it in favor of another kind of life, of which he
has, at the moment, only the dimmest apprehension.
Thus the movement of the novel is from the old house
—the house of youth, the house of life, the house of
artistic creation—by way of the temptation of the house
of success, to the new house of religious awareness.

Early in the novel St. Peter links art and religion
("they are the same thing, in the end, of course" [p.
69]) and separates them from science (i.e., technology).
Throughout the course of St. Peter's adult life, technology and all that is associated with it—expediency,
progress, materialism—have steadily gained ascendency
over artistic and, implicitly, religious values. The university, once the preserver of culture and art, is being
undermined and vulgarized by "the new comercialism,
the aim to 'show results.' " St. Peter has been one of the
few who have resisted this trend, though almost at
the cost of being squeezed out of his job by his political
enemies. The new direction of the world is clear, and
"the liberal appropriations, the promotions and in-
creases in salary, all went to the professors who worked
with the regents to abolish the purely cultural studies"
(p. 140).

Stated abstractly, it is easy to see the superiority
of the old world view, in which "every man and
woman who crowded into the cathedrals on Easter
Sunday was a principal in a gorgeous drama with
God," over the new, sterile technological era, which has
produced greater material comforts but which is spiritually destitute. But the concrete realities of life are
much more complex, and in *The Professor's House*

Willa Cather created a far more subtle and existentially valid situation than she had ever done before. In *A Lost Lady* it is too easy to despise Ivy Peters as a representative of the money-oriented modern world. But Louie Marsellus is not despicable, and St. Peter's discomfort with the Marsellus way of life comes down more to a difference in temperament than to a black-and-white contrast between materialism and artistic idealism. Louie in his own way is unquestionably generous, loving, compassionate, and long-suffering. While one may sometimes question his taste, one cannot question his good motives. His money has not corrupted him, but merely enabled him to be his most extravagant, generous self, and his enjoyment of his wealth is completely innocent.

But the other members of the professor's family, who have been nurtured in the tradition of art and have participated at least indirectly in the world of creative endeavor represented by St. Peter and Tom Outland, have been corrupted by Louie's money. They have let go of their old loyalties and ideals for a variety of reasons, all justifiable when regarded in one light but all ultimately bad. Kathleen wrongs her sister by resenting her marriage to Marsellus; Rosamund wrongs Kathleen by flaunting her wealth in the face of Kathleen's relative poverty; Scott wrongs Louie by his jealousy; and Lillian wrongs St. Peter by her marked preference for her son-in-law's way of life over his. The picture that emerges is in one sense very ordinary: a handful of petty rivalries and ambitions that seems counterbalanced by the genuine affection within each marital relationship, even that of St. Peter and Lillian. Given this situation, St. Peter's existential conflict becomes very ambiguous indeed.

Having thus created the emotional atmosphere in which St. Peter lives in Book I, Willa Cather introduced in Book II the sharp contrast of Tom Outland's discovery of the Blue Mesa. Some years after the publication of the novel she explained its unusual structure. She wanted, she said, to try two experiments in form: first, to insert the *"nouvelle"* (the self-contained story) into the body of the novel, after the fashion of early French and Spanish writers; second, to create an effect like that often found in Dutch paintings, in which the warm interior of a well-furnished kitchen or drawing room is set off by a square window open to the sea.

I tried to make Professor St. Peter's house rather over-crowded and stuffy with new things; American proprieties, clothes, furs, petty ambitions, quivering jealousies—until one got rather stifled. Then I wanted to open the square window and let in the fresh air that blew off the Blue Mesa, and the fine disregard of trivialities which was in Tom Outland's face and in his behaviour.[2]

Tom Outland's story is based on the actual discovery of the cliff dwellings in Mesa Verde by Dick Wetherell, a young cowboy who "forded the river and rode into the Mesa after lost cattle."[3] On one of her trips to the southwest, Willa Cather was fortunate enough to hear Wetherell's story from his brother, by that time a very old man. As she did in *The Song of the Lark,* Willa Cather used the cliff dwellings as a symbol of all that is of enduring value, in contrast to the ugliness and pettiness and essential heartlessness of modern society. As Thea finds in the fragments of the Indian pottery that vaguely articulated "desire" that is the source of all creativity, Tom finds in the cliff dwell-

ings a beauty to which his whole being responds, and
he gives himself wholeheartedly to efforts for their
preservation.

There is an implicit contrast between all the
houses in Book I—the run-down old house, the new
house with all of the modern conveniences, the pretentious copy of a Norwegian manor house being built
by the Marselluses—and the houses of the cliff dwellers.
The new houses are neither organically related to their
surroundings nor truly beautiful.

Even stronger is the implicit contrast between the
beautiful little city of stone and that other city of
monuments, Washington, D.C., where Tom goes in
search of government aid to excavate and properly
preserve the cliff dwellers' home and relics. Though
long dead, the ancient Indians are almost palpably
alive to Tom, and through their artifacts he senses that
they were a "strong and aspiring people . . . with a
feeling for design" (pp. 203–204). They were careful
craftsmen, patient and deliberate, developing their
primitive arts, observing religious ceremonials, making
their mesa "more and more worthy to be a home for
man" (p. 220). In contrast with this, the living city of
Washington is inhabited by pompous bureaucrats in-
different to everything but social prestige and prefer-
ment, or anxious civil servants who "spent their lives
trying to keep up appearances" (p. 232), or clerks pouring out of the government buildings at closing time
who seem to Tom "like people in slavery, who ought
to be free" (p. 234).

"Tom Outland's Story" gives the professor's story
a wider outlook; it is not merely that the professor's
personal life has become stifling to him, but that his
personal situation is a metaphor of the ills of the so-

ciety at large. Tom's frustration in Washington is
thematically parallel to St. Peter's losing battle with
the state legislature over the matter of the liberal arts
curriculum at the university. Both Tom and St. Peter
suffer from the indifference of the political world to
the preservation of culture, of things that have little
or no material value but are man's link with the past:
in the case of the liberal arts, man's link with all of
Western civilization; in the case of the Indian artifacts,
the American's link with the virtually unknown past
of his own continent. The Indians "built themselves
into [their] mesa and humanized it" (p. 221), but modern civilization, with its disregard for humane values
in its pursuit of materialism, is dehumanizing. Neither
St. Peter's city of Hamilton nor Washington, D.C.—
significantly the capital of the country—is especially
worthy "to be a home for man."

As Louie Marsellus's money is the source of most
of the problems within St. Peter's immediate orbit,
money is also the cause of the rift between Tom and
his companion Roddy Blake. Having guessed from
Tom's letters that no funds would be coming from
Washington, Roddy innocently sells the relics he and
Tom have collected to a German archeologist who
smuggles them out of the country. Tom, to whom the
artifacts are a priceless inheritance not to be sold for
money in the first place and certainly not to be sold to
a foreign country, is so overcome by anger that he
drives his friend away. Roddy, in his unthinking as-
sumption that the artifacts are in the same category as
a "gold mine or a pocket of turquoise" (p. 245) is not
being either mercenary or self-seeking; he is simply not
aware that they have a value to Tom that cannot be
measured in dollars and cents. But Roddy's assump-

tions are important, because they reflect the assumptions of society as a whole. Roddy always supposed that
Tom "meant to 'realize' on them . . . and that it
would come to money in the end. 'Everything does,' he
added" (p. 244).

Roddy is right, as the incidents in Book I show.
All that Tom was has "turned out chemicals and dollars
and cents" (p. 132) for everyone except St. Peter and
Kathleen. Even Professor Crane, Tom's dedicated and
idealistic physics teacher, has been infected by greed
for the money Tom's invention has brought the Marselluses, and complains aggrievedly: "Marsellus gets
the benefit of my work as well as of Outland's. I have
certainly been ill-used" (p. 148). But money per se is
only a symptom, a symbol, of the underlying disease,
a spiritual malaise that is so pervasive and protean that
a single name cannot be given to it. One merely sees its
effects: greed, jealousy, spitefulness, snobbery, vanity.
The effect of the square window letting in the fresh air
from the mesa is not only to introduce the clarity and
harmoniousness of the cliff dwellings but also to point
up, by the very contrast, the stuffiness and bad air of
the professor's dwellings.

Thus, when we come back to the professor's house
in Book III the original problem is brought into sharp
and personal focus. St. Peter has excused himself from
accompanying his wife and the Marselluses on a trip
to Europe and, left alone, retreats back into the old
house completely, smuggling in his bed and clothing.
There he reverts, not back to the immediate past of his
friendship with Tom Outland, but back to his own
almost forgotten boyhood, to his elemental, solitary
self that existed before the "secondary social man"
supplanted it. This boy was never involved in the web

of human relationships and worldly pursuits; he was a primitive who "was only interested in earth and woods and water. . . . He seemed to be at the root of the matter; Desire under all desires, Truth under all truths. . . . He was earth, and would return to earth" (p. 265). Concurrently with the emergence of his boyhood self, St. Peter comes to feel that he is near the end of his life.

Both the emergence of his boyhood self and his seeming drift toward death are puzzling and difficult to deal with if taken literally; they seem to suggest a kind of Freudian regression to childhood or prenatal unconsciousness in the face of insoluble difficulties in adult life. I find this interpretation both psychologically and artistically unsatisfying, for it does not take into account the significance of St. Peter's rescue from death by Augusta, the sewing woman. Such an interpretation would also make of the novel a deeply pessimistic testimony on the part of the author.

Leon Edel has argued that this novel is indeed a testimony of despair, written out of Willa Cather's feeling that life had become "static and despairing once she achieved her goals."[4] Whereas earlier "her theme had been power and conquest, it had become frustration and death."[5] Certainly Willa Cather, as she said in the preface to *The Song of the Lark,* found success in itself less interesting than the struggle for it, and like St. Peter, she actively tried to avoid becoming the kind of person that success tends to make of those who achieve it. Nevertheless, her theme does not then become "frustration and death," though she does something in some respects similar to that: she re-creates the post-World War I wasteland of materialism and spiritual sterility to which T. S. Eliot and others have testi-

fied. But out of her wasteland, like Eliot's, the protagonist can find fragments to shore against his ruins; the
scene is not unrelieved frustration and death, without
hope of resurrection.

It seems to me that the emergence of St. Peter's
boyhood self is indicative, not of his regression to a
more primitive level of consciousness, but of his in-
cipient rebirth. According to the psychologist C. G.
Jung, the figure of the child is a symbol of a new and
as yet unknown integration of the self that is emerging
out of intense psychic conflict and that signifies "a
higher stage of self-realization."[6] The archetype of the
child has a redemptive significance, for it comes from
beyond the limitations of the conscious personality and
possesses "a wholeness which embraces the very depths
of Nature."[7] As the child archetype symbolizes the
whole nature of man, it reaches back to the precon-
scious life of early childhood and forward to "an
anticipation by analogy of life after death."[8] An irra-
tional force, it represents "the strongest, the most
ineluctable urge in every being, namely, the urge to
realize itself. It is, as it were, an incarnation of *the
inability to do otherwise, equipped with all the powers
of nature and instinct,* whereas the conscious mind is
always getting caught in its supposed ability to do
otherwise."[9]

St. Peter's situation is strikingly similar to this
description. He seems bewildered, as though he were
not fully aware of all the implications involved in the
way he feels; he acts more out of intuitive, compelling
feelings than reasoned decisions. He does not understand why his child self emerges, and when he senses
the nearness of death he interprets his feeling literally.
He is surprised when a medical examination reveals

nothing wrong with him. He senses, in some obscure
way, that death is necessary and inevitable. This awareness of death has three different levels of meaning.
First, it signifies his mature acceptance of the reality of
death as a part of life, something which he has heretofore resisted in his attachment to the joys of life and
his shrinking from life's end. Second, he begins to see
that death is the metaphysical, not merely biological,
end of the kind of life he has led. It is "that house"—
the coffin, the house of death—to which the professor's
house—his life—is inexorably leading. But third, the
death he is about to undergo is a spiritual experience,
the death that is necessary for the birth of the new
man. He is in the process of conversion, of "turning
away" from all that he has been. In this light, I think,
his turning away from the man he has been—lover,
father, scholar—toward his boyhood self becomes a
meaningful metaphor.

The religious world view toward which St. Peter
is striving, almost unknown to himself, is ambiguous.
We glimpse it first in the person of Augusta, the Catholic sewing woman. Reliable, methodical, and very
devout, she seems at first to be a rather drab and not
especially compelling figure. Were it not for St. Peter's
obvious regard for her, one would perhaps dismiss her
as unimportant. She nevertheless has about her a faint
echo of some stern mythic figure. There is something
in her that, to St. Peter, suggests "the taste of bitter
herbs . . . the bloomless side of life that he had always run away from" (p. 280). She is a representative of
a religious view of life, but she is veiled under the most
commonplace and somber garments. Though St. Peter
jokes about her influence bringing him back to the
religion of his Catholic forebears, her way of life is

scarcely an obvious alternative to him in his present dilemma. If St. Peter is, indeed, to find his way back to the religion of his fathers, it will be no easy journey.

Learning that Lillian and the Marselluses are already en route for home on the *Berengaria*, St. Peter falls into a panic at the prospect of having to live with his family again. He feels he must be alone and almost covets the eternal solitude of death. He is still bound, in spite of himself, to his family, or their return could not mean so much to him. Faced with this insoluble problem—he cannot live with them, and he cannot separate himself from them—he subconsciously courts the "accident" that his faulty gas stove has long threatened. He falls asleep on his couch, and the wind blows out the stove and blows the window shut. Rescued from asphyxiation by the fortuitous arrival of Augusta, he finds that his symbolic death has changed him: "His temporary release from consciousness seemed to have been beneficial. He had let something go—and it was gone: something very precious, that he could not consciously have relinquished, probably" (p. 282).

Willa Cather was never specific as to precisely what it is he has let go; but that "something very precious" can only be all of his past life, his past self, his lifelong attachments: a true "letting go with the heart." It is no easy task, and its rewards are not immediately obvious. St. Peter returns to consciousness to the sight of Augusta, wrapped in her shawl, reading a much-worn religious book, and finds in her presence a quiet comfort: "Seasoned and sound and on the solid earth she surely was. . . . He even felt a sense of obligation toward her, instinctive, escaping definition, but real. And when you admitted that a thing was real, that was enough—now" (p. 281). One solid symbol of reality—

matter-of-fact and unglamorous and unexciting—is the only indication Willa Cather gives in this novel of the path St. Peter is taking. Just Augusta: no sign yet of the "gorgeous drama with God" that is implicit in religious faith. The horizons of Augusta's meaning shimmer just a little with hidden brightness as St. Peter, freed of his old life, contemplates "a world full of Augustas, with whom one was outward bound" (p. 281).

9

My

Mortal

Enemy

(1926)

My *Mortal Enemy* has been virtually ignored by Willa Cather's critics, who regard it either as unimportant (in the same class as *Alexander's Bridge*) or important only in the sense of revealing the pessimism and negativity that are frequently believed to have overtaken her after 1922. It is, certainly, a difficult and intransigent book, and Myra Henshawe is a difficult and contradictory character.

To the young narrator, Nellie Birdseye, Myra is an almost legendary figure:

I first met Myra Henshawe when I was fifteen, but I had known about her ever since I could remember anything at all. She and her runaway marriage were the theme of the most interesting, indeed the only interesting, stories that were told in our family [p. 9].*

Myra, to Nellie, is the very embodiment of romance. The niece and heiress of John Driscoll, the wealthiest man in Parthia, Illinois, Myra had everything—money, good looks, high spirits. But she fell in love with Oswald Henshawe, against whose family her uncle harbored an old grudge. She ran away to marry him in the face of her uncle's warning that he would disinherit her, as he did, leaving his money to the Catholic church and to charity. Young Nellie is not the only one caught up in the romance that Myra's story seems to radiate; to Nellie's Aunt Lydia, Myra's contemporary and friend, that "thrilling night" when Myra ran away to marry Oswald was "probably the most exciting in her life" (p. 23). But when Nellie asks if the Henshawes have been happy, Aunt Lydia only surmises that they have been as happy as most people. To Nellie, "that

* Page references in this discussion are to *My Mortal Enemy* (New York: Alfred A. Knopf, 1926).

88

answer was disheartening; the very point of their story was that they should be much happier than other people" (p. 25).

After a brief meeting with the Henshawes in Parthia, Nellie and Aunt Lydia are invited to visit them in New York at Christmastime. To the raw western girl, New York City at the turn of the century is magical, and everything from the Henshawes' beautifully appointed apartment to their theatrical and literary friends fills her with wonder and admiration. The visit ends on a discordant note, however. Nellie comes across the Henshawes quarreling, Myra being high-handed and tyrannical, Oswald in his own way giving back as good as he gets. Nellie is stricken to see the kindness and courtesy of her friends give way to this and feels that she can never care for Myra so much again.

Ten years later Nellie, down on her luck, is living in a shabby residential hotel on the west coast and discovers among her neighbors Oswald, now white-haired and stoop-shouldered, and Myra, incurably ill. To Nellie's distress, when Myra is overwrought she takes her feelings out on the devoted Oswald, saying that they have destroyed each other and that she ought never to have married him.

After she enters the terminal stage of her illness, Myra talks very little, and when she does speak it seems to be more a vocalization of an inner dialogue with herself than words addressed to those with her. One night Myra murmurs, "Why must I die like this, alone with my mortal enemy?" (p. 113). After an initial reaction of shock, Nellie thinks that she begins to understand "a little what she meant, to sense how it was with her. Violent natures like hers sometimes turn against themselves . . . against themselves and

all their idolatries." The following night, left alone
briefly, Myra disappears, leaving a note to Oswald that
she has gone off to die alone. When she is found the
next morning, on a cliff overlooking the sea where she
had sometimes gone with Nellie, she is dead.

The most radically *démeublé* of Willa Cather's
novels, *My Mortal Enemy* is stripped of virtually all
descriptive detail. Except for the scenes in New York,
even the setting, ordinarily so much a part of her writing, is reduced to the merest suggestion. Parthia, Illinois, is scarcely more than a name on a map, and the
west coast locale of the final pages is characterized by
little more than a shabby hotel and a promontory overlooking the sea. The novel has the economy of drama
and recalls the desire Willa Cather expressed in "The
Novel Démeublé" to "leave the room as bare as the
stage of a Greek theatre . . . for the play of emotions,
great and little."[1] It is her working out of the principle
expressed by the elder Dumas, who said that "to make
a drama, a man needed one passion, and four walls."[2]

Willa Cather's method of evoking that one passion
is through conflict. Though the conflict is given its visible expression in terms of Myra's love-enmity relationship with her husband, we should be careful not to
interpret this too literally, for the essential conflict is
within Myra herself. This is reflected in the contradictory aspects of Myra's personality: she is capable of
deep tenderness and great scorn, she is both generous
and unforgiving, she is at one moment condescending
to the rich friends she cultivates on Oswald's account
and at another bitterly resentful of her own relative
poverty. These contradictions force us out of our normal tendency to try to understand and account for

character and make us focus on the impenetrable mystery of character itself. Insofar as Willa Cather is successful (and the difficulty that readers have with the novel indicate that her success is only partial), Myra Henshawe becomes not merely the embodiment of conflict but a sharply realized character whose reality exists beyond analysis and who mysteriously exerts a compelling power over us.

Willa Cather develops another aspect of conflict in the juxtaposition of the young, romantic narrator, Nellie, with a dying woman who had been a romantic in her youth, a woman who had thrown away money, religion, family, all for love, and who found that love was not enough. Nellie is sympathetic enough to be touched by Myra's bitter disillusionment with love, but she is also sensitive to the compelling attractiveness of a love story, in which a "common feeling [is] exalted into beauty by imagination, generosity, and the flaming courage of youth" (p. 122). Thus, Willa Cather presented two deeply felt and contradictory aspects of life: the "flaming courage of youth," which she found so beautiful and which she celebrated in *O Pioneers!* and *My Ántonia;* and the discovery, which comes with age and the awareness of death, that love is inadequate.

The theme of the inadequacy of love is sounded very early in the book, with Nellie's hearing that Myra and Oswald, after their romantic beginning, have not been happier than most people. When Nellie meets her in New York Myra is in the company of Ewan Gray, a young man in love with an actress friend of hers. Oswald remarks, soon after, that "Myra is so fond of helping young men along. We nearly always have a love affair on hand" (p. 30). Myra immediately denies it; she has sworn never to meddle in love affairs again. But she is torn between her romantic attraction to love and her growing realization of its shortcomings:

"You send a handsome fellow like Ewan Gray to a fine girl like Esther, and it's Christmas eve, and they rise above us and the white world around us, and there isn't anybody . . . that wouldn't wish them well—and very likely hell will come of it!" [p. 41].

In the last section, dealing with Myra's illness, love is seen as not only disillusioning but potentially destructive, as Myra learns of the suicide of a young actor because of "some sordid love affair."

Various literary allusions in the novel suggest that, out of love for Oswald, Myra left behind the life in which she had been raised and thereby in some way violated her own nature. This is underscored by the scene of Myra's New Year's party at which an opera singer gives a spontaneous and deeply moving rendition of the aria "Casta Diva" ("chaste goddess") from the opera *Norma.* Nellie dwells on the relationship between that aria and Myra:

For many years I associated Mrs. Henshawe with that music, thought of that aria as being mysteriously related to some-thing in her nature that one rarely saw, but nearly always felt; a compelling, passionate, overmastering something for which I had no name, but which was audible, visible, in the air that night. . . . When I wanted to recall powerfully that hidden richness in her, I had only to close my eyes and sing to myself: "casta diva, casta diva!" [pp. 60–61].

Myra is thus associated with the Druidic high priestess Norma, who has broken her vows of chastity for love of a Roman soldier, an enemy of her people. (Nellie, on another occasion, reflects that Oswald's life as a businessman has not suited him, that he ought to have been a soldier or an explorer.) As love is a betrayal of Norma's vows, in some undefined way it is also a betrayal for Myra, for the "compelling, passionate, overmastering something" in her nature cannot be satisfied in the marital relationship, and may, indeed, be the explanation of Myra's tyrannical jealousy: she is unconsciously demanding something of a human love that it cannot be expected to satisfy. It is, for her, an idolatry—the worship of a false god.

Richard Giannone has suggested that Myra's passion is for immortality.[3] In terms of the images used in the novel, Myra has sought to fulfill her desire in things outside herself—in Oswald, in her friendships, in material beauty and elegance, in the theater and art—and has found them unsatisfying. Poetry, she feels, is immortal ("How the great poets do shine on. . . . They have no night" [p. 99]), but she is not a poet. She is an artist only in being herself, and to fully become herself she must return to her sources, symbolized by her fierce old uncle and the Catholic faith of her childhood. Religion, she finds, "is different from everything else; *because in religion seeking is finding*" (p. 111). For her, religion is both the means and the expression of wholeness, of becoming one with herself. Thus, in spite of her unsaintlike qualities—her arrogance, her hatred of poverty—the intensity of her passion for wholeness, for immortality, is such that Father Fay remarks, "I wonder whether some of the saints of the early Church weren't a good deal like her" (p. 111).

Though Myra's conflict is ended by her death, the conflict which underlies the novel as a whole is not resolved; Nellie concludes her narration some years after Myra's death, still torn between her attraction to the beauty of love and Myra's testimony as to its inadequacy. The novel thus seems to be an experiment in the depiction of conflict in an almost pure form, and the problems of understanding its meaning have stemmed from focusing too much on, and trying to make satisfactory sense out of, the particulars in which the conflict is expressed. The whole refractoriness of the novel, its resistance to resolution, seems to be Willa Cather's attempt to forestall the natural tendency to thrust past conflict toward resolution. Instead she would have us remain, almost against our will, in the conflict situation itself, until we not only experience it in its particular form, the powerful and discomforting relationship between Myra and her mortal enemy, but also recognize that it points to an unspecific, elemental conflict within the human soul.

10

Death Comes

for the

Archbishop

(1927)

Though radically different in technique from her obviously *démeublé* novels *A Lost Lady* and *My Mortal Enemy*, the essence of *Death Comes for the Archbishop* is *démeublé* in its evocation of mood and its creation of all that is "felt upon the page without being specifically named there." Willa Cather herself said of the *Archbishop* that "the mood is the thing—all the little figures and stories are mere improvisations that come out of it."[1] The predominant mood is that of faith: the belief in a transcendent reality which gives meaning and order to human life. The note of faith is sounded on the narrative level in the simple fact that the two main characters are priests, whose lives are grounded in faith; and that note reverberates throughout the novel. It is a part of the emotional penumbra which is both created by the narrative level and which gives to the narrative its sometimes almost numinous quality.

The background of the *Archbishop* Willa Cather gained from her several trips to the southwest, during which she not only explored the country but became fascinated by its history and especially by the role played by the Catholic church. Just as she had drawn upon a Dutch pictorial model of an interior with a square window opening on the sea in *The Professor's House*, Willa Cather again adapted the techniques of painting in *Death Comes for the Archbishop*. Here she used as her model the murals on the walls of the Pantheon in Paris of the life of Saint Geneviève, by the nineteenth-century French painter Puvis de Chavannes. These Chavannes murals, in two groups of four panels each, depict the French saint at different stages in her life. They convey a strong feeling of order and tranquility and are characterized by a simplicity of line and delicate harmony of color. Though the scenes are static, they are charged with a sense of quiet momentousness, and an impression of movement is created by the eye as it moves from panel to panel. In much the same way, movement in the *Archbishop* is from episode to episode. The nine books of the novel might well be compared to nine tableaux in which the figures of Father Latour and/or Father Vaillant are central but which are filled with a variety of other characters —some drawn but once, others reappearing in later scenes—all depicted with a Chavannes-like simplicity of line and immediacy of characterization.

Chavannes's work, curiously enough, stands in much the same relation to the better-known impressionists, who were his contemporaries, as does the work of Willa Cather to the more influential writers of the 1920s. According to Clinton Keeler,

when the impressionists were directing the point of view of art further inward [to the eye itself, the breaking up of light in the act of seeing], Puvis de Chavannes went back to an earlier period [the Florentine Renaissance] for the clarity of individual figures . . . their flatness and their lack of accent.[2]

Similarly, "writing at a time when the innovation of Joyce and others had led fiction *within* the mind, within the process of consciousness, Cather turned to an earlier period,"[3] to historical subjects and a classical style.

Death Comes for the Archbishop shows classical influences not only in the restraint and clarity of its style but in one of its underlying motifs as well. The classical allusions are the merest suggestions, never obtrusive, but they provide the key to one of several sym-

bolic levels which give the narrative its depth and
power. Thus, in the prologue, set in Rome in 1848,
three cardinals and a bishop discuss the founding of
an apostolic vicarate in the territory of New Mexico,
which the United States has recently acquired. The
task of the new bishop of New Mexico will be a heroic
one: to be shepherd to the Mexican population and to
the thirty Indian nations that inhabit the vast, primitive desert country, and to cleanse the "Augean sta-
bles" of laxness and abuses that have grown up among
the native clergy since the evangelization of the southwest by the Franciscan Fathers in the 1500s.

The metaphor of the heroic undertaking is continued in Book I, which opens with the newly consecrated bishop, Jean-Marie Latour, en route alone on
horseback from Santa Fe to Durango in Old Mexico.
On his arrival at Santa Fe, the Mexican priests had
refused to recognize his authority, since his credentials
had not been sent from the Bishop of Durango. To
prove himself worthy of his task, he undertakes the
ordeal of the three-thousand-mile round-trip journey
across trackless desert in order to bring his credentials
back himself.

The theme of the heroic undertaking here merges
with the journey motif, which in the course of the
novel reappears in several forms, most of which involve
leaving one's familiar world to create a new life in a
new land. This is, essentially, the same journey as the
pioneer journey celebrated in *O Pioneers!* and *My
Ántonia,* and Bishop Latour, like the protagonists in
those novels, is setting out to create order out of the
formlessness of a wild and half-pagan land. As I have
noted in the discussion of *O Pioneers!*, the settling of
a new country is a symbolic reenactment of the Crea-

tion. As such, it is an act that implies an awareness of the sacred, which in the pioneer novels is primarily expressed as an awareness of the awesome power and enrapturing beauty of nature. For religious man,[4] all of nature and all created things are a possible medium through which, from time to time, the sacred—which can be experienced as a sense of power, of being, of heightened reality—manifests itself.

In *Death Comes for the Archbishop* this generalized religious awareness is given a specifically Christian form and expressed through Christian symbolism. Its thematic importance in the novel is stressed in each of the four sections of Book I. Thus, in "The Cruciform Tree" the bishop, lost in an endless waste of sandhills, suddenly comes upon a juniper tree grown in the shape of a cross. To him it is not an oddity nor merely a sign which reminds him of his religious faith, but a clear revelation of the sacred in a natural object. The universe, to him, is not opaque and meaningless, but transparent to ultimate reality, and his simple actions are charged with power and meaning because they not only spring from him but also have reference to a sacred model. Thus, as he rides on after his devotions at the foot of the cruciform tree, he suffers excruciatingly from thirst. Remembering Christ, who cried on the cross, "I thirst!" he "blotted himself out of his own consciousness and meditated upon the anguish of his Lord" (p. 20).*

The connection between the transcendent realm and the world of men is emphasized in the scene at Hidden Water, an isolated village upon which the lost

* Page references in this discussion are to *Death Comes for the Archbishop* (New York: Vintage Books, 1971).

Bishop Latour stumbles. The spot itself—a tiny oasis nourished by a subterranean stream in the midst of desolation—seems to be one of those places in which men instinctively recognize the sacred. The bishop musingly compares it to "those well-heads in his own country where the Roman settlers had set up the image of a river goddess, and later Christian priests had planted a cross" (p. 32). The settlement is inhabited by pious Mexicans who have not had a priest in their midst for generations and who regard the appearance of Bishop Latour as miraculous: "the Blessed Virgin must have led the Bishop from his path and brought him here to baptize the children and to sanctify the marriages" (p. 26). These primitive Mexicans are deeply aware of the interrelationship between earth and heaven; thus a young villager tells the bishop of his name saint, Santiago, who is the patron saint of horses: "He blesses the mares and makes them fruitful. Even the Indians believe that. They know that if they neglect to pray to Santiago for a few years, the foals do not come right" (p. 29).

Bishop Latour returns from Mexico with his credentials to find a warm welcome in Santa Fe, where his vicar, Father Vaillant, has "already endeared himself to the people." As the bishop's general task of establishing order and discipline in his diocese is an archetypal act symbolically equivalent to the divine creation of the cosmos out of primordial chaos, so his establishment of his house in Santa Fe is a similar symbolic act of Creation. Because of their awareness of the sacred, even the household duties of the bishop and his vicar take on a depth and an almost numinous quality of reality. Willa Cather's emphasis on the importance of the salad in the civilizing of a country is no mere

whimsy, but a valid metaphor of the sacramentaliza-
tion of the act of eating, which, along with birth, marriage, and death, is one of the vital experiences of human existence. The whole of life is truly capable of
being sanctified,[5] as is reflected in Bishop Latour's
remark that their burning cedar logs give off such a
sweet aroma that "At our meanest tasks we have a
perpetual odour of incense about us" (p. 35).

Book I concludes with a clear irruption of the
transcendent into the human world in the story of
the apparition of the Virgin at Guadalupe in 1531,
the only "absolutely authenticated appearance of the
Blessed Virgin in the New World" (p. 46). Though it
occurred in the past, the apparition belongs to a timeless reality that can be reentered from any point in
historical time. Thus, the devout priest who has just
made a pilgrimage to Guadalupe has symbolically
experienced the apparition himself and returns "full
of the sweetness of his late experience" and "so rapt
that nothing else interested him" (p. 46). The miracle
is a tangible experience of the sacred. Even more, as
Father Latour expresses it, "an apparition is human
vision corrected by divine love" (p. 50); in other words,
when one sees the sacred revealed, one sees what has
always been there all along—one sees reality. The
bishop concludes:

"The Miracles of the Church seem to me to rest not so
much upon faces or voices or healing power coming suddenly near to us from afar off, but upon our perceptions
being made finer, so that for a moment our eyes can see and
our ears hear what is there about us always" [p. 50].

Thus Book I establishes the themes that underlie the
narrative: the transcendent as the source of reality and

the interconnectedness between the material world and the spiritual world.

The journey motif with which Book I opens continues throughout the novel, given expression both in the bishop's journey to the end of his life and in the particular physical journeys that he undertakes during the course of it. The adventures, in Book II, of the two priests as they travel throughout the diocese are again suggestive of the adventures of the classical heroes; while one would not call Father Vaillant cunning or wily, there is a touch of the craftiness of Odysseus in his obtaining from the rich Mexican Manuel Lujon the gift of two splendid cream-colored mules. The subhuman creature Buck Scales, who murders travelers who stop at his shack on the lonely road to Mora, is reminiscent of the many legendary outlaws whose habit it is to murder their guests. The priests escape, warned by Scales's terrified wife, and their encounter with him leads indirectly to the outlaw's capture and execution.

Books III through V continue the theme of the bishop's task as stated in the prologue: like Odysseus returning to set to rights his household, Bishop Latour is to bring order and discipline to a diocese long without guidance, to suspend the dissolute clergy and to reward those who have been faithful to their office. The Homeric parallel is further suggested in the way Willa Cather echoes the Homeric epithet (e.g., "rosy-fingered dawn" or "ox-eyed Hera") in the beautiful descriptions of the missions the bishop intends to visit: "Santo Domingo, breeder of horses; Isleta, whitened with gypsum; Laguna, of wide pastures; and finally, cloud-set Ácoma" (p. 82).

In section 3 of Book III the mythic level emerges again, although in a somewhat different form from that in which it appeared earlier: here what is suggested is not the timelessness of the sacred breaking through into the world of the present, but the anachronistic survival of the primordial chaos that existed before the creation. Thus the bishop reflects on the appearance of the mesa country, which seems to have a great antiquity and incompleteness "as if, with all the materials for world-making assembled, the Creator had desisted, gone away and left everything on the point of being brought together, on the eve of being arranged into mountain, plain, plateau" (p. 95).

The Indians who inhabit the Ácoma mesa seem to have persisted unchanged, like a fossil form of life, through all the centuries during which man and his history have been evolving. Bishop Latour likens them to rock-turtles on their rock, and feels in them something reptilian, "something that had endured by immobility, a kind of life out of reach, like the crustaceans in their armour" (p. 103). This section suggests that, however much man may yearn for stability and safety and seek through symbolic and ritual behavior to reestablish contact with the timeless and the sacred, he must not therefore refuse to move forward with time and accomplish his evolutionary destiny. This destiny in the case of the Ácomas is not, of course, to be assimilated to the white man's ways and thus enter secular history, but to continue to develop from the condition of rock-turtles to something more fully approaching the potentiality of man.

Another arrested stage of evolutionary development is suggested by the Pecos Indians in Book IV. Once rich and populous, the Pecos tribe is dying out. Their decline is suggestively linked with dark legends of snake worship. Willa Cather develops the image of the snake as a symbol of darkness and chaos[6] in the episode in which Bishop Latour and his Pecos guide, Jacinto, take refuge during a storm in a secret ceremonial cave. Though no snake manifests itself, Jacinto's mysterious behavior suggests that the cave is the dwelling of a creature which he regards with dread and religious awe.

Despite the fact that the cave offers him safety from the storm and probably saves his life, the bishop feels an extreme distaste for it. He seems to sense that he is in the presence of some nameless and formless horror, something too abysmal to be articulated but graphically symbolized in the unseen snake and in the sound of the underground river flowing through a cavern far beneath the cave. Both the snake and the dark waters are the equivalents, on the mythic plane, of the chaos existing before Creation that Bishop Latour saw in the physical landscape of Ácoma. As the Ácoma Indians suggest an arrested stage of evolutionary development in time, the Pecos suggest an arrested religious development; though their dread worship of chaos supported their lives in the past, they have failed to grow beyond it, and it is symbolically draining the life force away from them.

The incidents in Book V suggest the continuation of evolutionary development in the historic present. Padre Martínez, the native priest who is the virtual ruler of Taos, belongs to an "age of lawless personal power" that is now almost over, even on the frontier. Though Martínez is a masterful and impressive figure and is completely unwilling to surrender his power, Bishop Latour senses that he is "really impotent, left over from the past" (p. 141). The bishop is symbolically ushering in a new age, a new beginning, a new Creation; he is to bring order, form, and harmony to the chaos that is suggested on the mythical level by the Ácoma and Pecos Indians and that is graphically depicted in the slovenly condition of Padre Martínez's household.

The effects of this new Creation are expressed in terms of the consecration (or renewal) of space and of time. Book VI introduces the prime physical symbol of the new Creation, the cathedral which the bishop wishes to build. The building of a cathedral implies the regeneration of the world by consecrating it; by being brought in contact with the sacred, the world is symbolically created anew, *"as it was in the beginning, when it came fresh from the Creator's hands."*[7] There is a mythological connection between the renewal of the world, or of space, implicit in the building of a cathedral, and the renewal of sacred time symbolized in the celebration of the New Year.[8] Thus it is fitting that the announcement that the wealthy Spaniard Don Olivares intends to give a sum sufficient to enable the bishop to begin work on his cathedral occurs at the Olivares' New Year's party.

The theme of the consecration of space and of time is continued in Book VII, "The Great Diocese," as Bishop Latour's original diocese is expanded to include the vast territories to the south acquired by the United States in the Gadsden Purchase. The diocese itself—the territory for which the bishop is responsible —is analogous to the cathedral: it, too, is a space to be consecrated by the bishop's creative work on it. To make boundaries, to bring lands together by relating them to a central point (i.e., the episcopal city of Santa Fe) is to bring form out of formlessness.

Other scenes in Book VII suggest the renewal or

recovery of time. The season is spring, the time of the annual renewal of the year in the rebirth of vegetation; more than that, it is the time when "this sinful and sullied world" (i.e., the world of history) "puts on white as if to commemorate the Annunciation, and becomes, for a little, lovely enough to be in truth the Bride of Christ" (p. 204). The past breakthrough of the sacred into history (the annunciation) is annually made anew, and the culmination of the evolutionary process[9] that is still in the future (when the world will be the bride of Christ) is annually promised.

As sacred time is thus recovered in historical time, one's personal past is also recovered,[10] not simply remembered but reexperienced (as the annunciation is not simply commemorated but symbolically made present). Father Vaillant, musing in the bishop's garden on how the most important events in his own life had occurred in May, remembers the critical incident of his youth when he had been unable to bring himself to part from his family in order to embark on his life as a missionary: "That time came back upon Father Vaillant now so keenly that he wiped a little moisture from his eyes" (p. 205).

Finally, the perfection of sacred time, immediately after the Creation and before the Fall, is suggested in a beautiful image as Magdalena comes into the garden surrounded by a flock of doves which fly around her, settling on her arms and shoulders and eating from her hand. "When she put a crust of bread between her lips, two doves hung in the air before her face, stirring their wings and pecking at the morsel" (p. 210). The fact that the now-beautiful Magdelena was once the horribly abused wife of Buck Scales underscores the redemptive nature of the recovery of sacred time. Bishop

Latour's garden (his own creation, his only recreation) is indeed suggestive of paradise.

In Book VIII the renewal of space is continued in terms of the same images under which it appeared earlier: the cathedral and the addition of new territory to the bishop's jurisdiction, this time to the north. The episodes of Book VIII suggest an end and a new beginning: as the bishop's creative task is rounding toward completion, his dream of a cathedral—the physical symbol of his work—begins to be realized, and he takes Father Vaillant out to view the hill of ochre-colored rock from which the stone for his cathedral will be cut. Though the bishop's special task is almost accomplished, the creation of order out of chaos must be constantly renewed. When an urgent message arrives from the bishop of Leavenworth asking for a priest to be sent to the new gold-rush areas in the Colorado Rockies, the task is taken up by Father Vaillant. The new undertaking (which, in time, will make Father Vaillant the first bishop of Colorado) is not merely a repetition of Bishop Latour's work in New Mexico; the creative task is the same, but the world in which he is to act is very different. Instead of the traditional culture of the Mexicans and Indians of the southwest, which, like all primitive societies, is rooted in an awareness of the sacred, Father Vaillant is faced with a society that is prototypically modern in its rootlessness and in its scramble after material wealth. Drawn from all over the country, the gold seekers are without homes, families, or spiritual guidance. Their relationship to the earth is not sacramental, as is that of an agricultural people, but exploitive; because they are cut off from the sacred, their living conditions—symbolic of their very lives—are dehumanized.

The golden rock out of which the bishop intends to build his cathedral is implicitly contrasted with the gold-filled mountain which has suddenly drawn thousands of men to Colorado. The former is a physical symbol of transcendent reality and value whose function is to continually resanctify the world; the latter, so similar in description, is totally different in orientation, pointing not to the reality of the sacred but to the radical desacralization of nature and the loss of the transcendent. Father Vaillant's task to restore an awareness of the sacred to this alienated world is truly a heroic one.

Book IX is set in 1888, nearly thirty years after Father Vaillant's departure for Colorado. Father Vaillant is now dead. Bishop Latour has seen his cathedral completed, has been made archbishop, and has retired to a little country estate four miles from Santa Fe. Rather than spend his declining years in France, as he had once expected, he has chosen to live out his life in the southwest, where some quality of the air—a quality found only in new countries—makes him awake feeling like a boy again. Here the symbol of the new creation is expressed in two additional modes: in the physical landscape itself, and in the psychological effect it has on the retired archbishop. Whereas in the first eight books the renewal of space and the recovery of time were the symbolic results of Bishop Latour's creative action, in Book IX the new creation and the freedom from historical time are directly experienced by him. Moreover, he experiences them more as actualities than as metaphors: "In New Mexico he always awoke a young man; not until he rose and began to shave did he realize that he was growing older" (p. 275). His experience is full of images that suggest new, young life setting out into an uncharted and beautiful country: "His first consciousness was a sense of the light dry wind blowing in through the windows, with a fragrance of hot sun and sagebrush and sweet clover; a wind that made one's body feel light and one's heart cry out 'to-day, to-day,' like a child's" (p. 275). The wind—symbolically the creative spirit—of the new country restores his youth.

As the archbishop approaches death the literal New Mexico landscape and its mythic and paradisiacal prototype virtually become one; thus the novel's penultimate section describes the expulsion of the Navahos from their ancestral lands where their gods dwell, their cruel exile in a strange land, and finally their happy return "to their sacred places." Seeing the Navahos restored to their homelands, their sheep "grazing under the magnificent cottonwoods and drinking at the streams of sweet water," the archbishop likens the scene to "an Indian Garden of Eden" (p. 297). Though the archbishop's death is the end of his life on earth and the end of the novel as well, the images surrounding it—the new country, the Indian Garden of Eden—suggest that it is much less an end than a beginning. The sense of ongoingness is further emphasized through the metaphor of the journey. The archbishop's journey into death is interwoven with his memory of the story, recounted earlier, of how Jean-Marie Latour helped his young friend Joseph Vaillant make the courageous decision that was to take him away from home and family and begin his missionary life. Of course, in this final scene, the two figures in the story are both aspects of the archbishop himself:

he was trying to give consolation to a young man who was being torn in two before his eyes by the desire to go and the necessity to stay. He was trying to forge a new Will in that devout and exhausted priest; and the time was short, for the *diligence* for Paris was already rumbling down the mountain gorge [p. 299].

The death that comes for the archbishop is not a grim and grinning skeleton, as depicted in the Holbein woodcut[11] from which the novel takes its name, but a *diligence*—a carriage.

11

Shadows

on the Rock

(1931)

As in *Death Comes for the Archbishop,* the theme of *Shadows on the Rock* is the creation of order in a savage land. The story is centered in the household of the widowed apothecary Euclide Auclair and his twelve-year-old daughter, Cécile. Their day-to-day activities are devoted to the orderly carrying on of the French way of life in the Canadian wilderness in the late seventeenth century. Through the Auclairs' encounters with their friends and neighbors there emerges a vivid pictorial image of the rock of Quebec (Quebec is built on a rocky promontory) and its citizens, from the misshapen creature Blinker, whom the Auclairs befriend out of kindness, the little boy Jacques Gaux, to whom Cécile is half playmate and half mother, and the cobbler and his lame mother on Holy Family Hill, to the great figures such as the formidable Bishop Laval and the governor of Quebec himself, Count Frontenac.

The novel, which has no plot in the conventional sense, is a series of pictures, deftly sketched and more suggestive than complete, richly evocative of the feeling about life that had been preserved in Quebec through the centuries. At the root of that feeling about life is reverence for tradition, and especially for religious tradition. The colonists are exiled from their homes in France, cut off from their families and friends; but, like exiled Aeneas, they bring their gods with them:

Inferretque deos Latio. When an adventurer carries his gods with him into a remote and savage country, the colony he founds will, from the beginning, have graces, traditions, riches of the mind and spirit. Its history will shine with bright incidents, slight, perhaps, but precious, as in life itself, where the great matters are often as worthless as astronomical distances, and the trifles dear as the heart's blood [p. 98].*

The "trifles dear as the heart's blood" are the emotional substance of the novel, the day-to-day affairs that are expressed in episodes of simple but lambent beauty: the matter of salads, of preserving doves in lard for the winter, of fitting Jacques with a pair of shoes, of visiting the church or coasting down Holy Family Hill in winter. Interwoven with these vignettes are the narratives of the greater religious personages in the history of Quebec: the rivalry between old Bishop Laval and his arrogant young successor; the story of the recluse Jeanne Le Ber, who had been the richest heiress in Montreal and who immured herself for life in a cell behind the high altar of a nunnery chapel; the story of the suffering endured for the love of God by the missionary Noël Chabanel, martyred by the Iroquois fifty years before the time of the story.

As the first three books emphasize the religious foundations on which the colony of Quebec has been built, the last three focus on the secular life and the completion of the cycle of the year with which the story opened. Auclair and Cécile welcome the re-appearance of their old friend, the exuberant and daring fur trader Pierre Charron. Charron represents the new type of man, the true Canadian who is a product both of the culture of the Old World and of the Canadian forests. Cécile, too, embodies the traditions of France engrafted onto a new life in Quebec. After visiting the Harnois, a slovenly country family, she realizes that she does her domestic tasks so carefully

* Page references in this discussion are to *Shadows on the Rock* (New York: Alfred A. Knopf, 1931).

not merely to please her father or out of loyalty to her dead mother, but for herself:

These coppers, big and little, these brooms and clouts and brushes, were tools; and with them one made, not shoes or cabinet-work, but life itself. One made a climate within a climate; one made the days,—the complexion, the special flavour, the special happiness of each day as it passed; one made life [p. 198].

Cécile passes, at that moment of realization, from childhood to the beginnings of young womanhood, no longer a French exile but a new creature, a Quebecois, to whom the rock of Quebec is home because she has made life there.

A good portion of the novel is taken up with narratives of figures in Quebec's history or of events which occurred in France. Not only do these narratives provide background and place the colony of Quebec in the physical context of the great wilderness that surrounds it and in the historical context of the European world, but they also suggest a thematic contrast between two ways of life. On the one hand, there is, in addition to the self-sacrificing religious figures already mentioned, Mother Catherine de Saint-Augustin, who "at thirty-seven had burned her life out in vigils, mortifications, visions, raptures, all the while carrying on a steady routine of manual labour and administrative work" (p. 42). On the other hand, there are the figures whom no ideal inspires, such as the uncouth Harnois family or those who, like the ruling classes in Europe, put the protection of property before the values of human life —reflected, for example, in the law that allows a needy old man to be tortured and hanged for the theft of two brass pots.

It is easy to see the shortcomings of a regime which maintains law and order through torture or which demands flattery and a courtier's manner for political advancement; and for the average man—such as Auclair or Pierre Charron—it is difficult not to see the sacrifice of Noël Chabanel or Jeanne Le Ber as a waste and a loss. Auclair finally concludes that the seemingly wasteful sacrifice of the missionaries is like "the box of precious ointment which was acceptable to the Saviour, and I am like the disciples who thought it might have been better used in another way" (p. 155). Pierre Charron completely fails to understand that the sacrifice of his once-beloved Jeanne is anything but a tragedy for her and her family; but to Cécile and to nameless others the holy recluse and her miraculous visit from the angels is a source of great joy:

The word of her visit from the angels went abroad over snow-burdened Canada to the remote parishes. Wherever it went, it brought pleasure, as if the recluse herself had sent to all those families whom she did not know some living beauty,—a blooming rose-tree, or a shapely fruit-tree in fruit. Indeed, she sent them an incomparable gift. . . .

The people have loved miracles for so many hundred years, not as proof or evidence, but because they are the actual flowering of desire. In them the vague worship and devotion of the simple-hearted assumes a form. From being a shapeless longing, it becomes a beautiful image; a dumb rapture becomes a melody that can be remembered and repeated; and the experience of a moment, which might have been a lost ecstasy, is made an actual possession and can be bequeathed to another [p. 137].

Through these vignettes Willa Cather created a mood, a flavor of life, which suffuses the novel and makes deeply real the unobtrusive virtues out of which the Auclairs' life is built: loyalty, steadfastness, compassion, faith. Those virtues are also symbolized by the enduring rock of Quebec, across whose surface play the shadows of succeeding generations. In this symbol, contained in the title, is a dynamic metaphor of constancy and change: against the immutable and intangible ideals that are the bedrock on which the human community is built pass the individual human figures, subject to time and growth and change and death, and the movement of history itself.

12

~~~~~~~~~~~~~~~~~~~~~~~~~~~~~~~~~~~~~~~

Obscure

Destinies

(1932)

Shortly after her father's death in 1928, Willa Cather wrote "Neighbour Rosicky," the first of the three short stories collected in *Obscure Destinies*. Its central character was modeled after a Bohemian farmer, but for the circumstances of Rosicky's death, and probably for much of the feeling out of which the story was written, Willa Cather drew from the life and death of her own father.

The story is simple: Rosicky learns from the doctor that his heart is bad and he must no longer do heavy farm work. He had been a tailor in his youth, and now, confined to the house, he sews and remembers first his years in New York and then his earlier and more painful years as an immigrant in London. Interwoven with these memories is his present concern for his eldest son, Rudolph, and Rudolph's young American wife, Polly. Rosicky fears that Rudolph will quit his farm and go to work in Omaha, where he can make more money, because Polly, who was raised a town girl, is dissatisfied with farm life and feels stiff and uncomfortable with her husband's Bohemian family. Farm life has its crop failures and hardships, Rosicky knows, but they are nothing compared to the cruelty and human depravity he witnessed in the London streets.

A cold winter freezes the wheat in the ground, and a dry spring promises a hard year. Rosicky is concerned about thistles that have grown in his son's alfalfa field, and one morning when Rudolph is away the old man hitches up a team and rakes them up. The exertion brings on an attack, and he is taken into the house and cared for by a frightened Polly. Rosicky's affection for her and understanding of her bring her to a new awareness of herself and to a sudden recognition of her

118

father-in-law's gift for loving people. Rosicky, in his turn, discovers Polly's tender heart and knows that he need not worry about her and Rudolph any longer. The next day he suffers another attack and dies. Some weeks later the doctor, passing by the country graveyard where the old man is buried, muses that "Rosicky's life seemed to him complete and beautiful" (p. 71).*

"Neighbour Rosicky," for all its simplicity and seeming slightness of subject, is among the finest of Willa Cather's works. To create simple, believable, unself-consciously good characters is enormously difficult; but neighbor Rosicky, with his warm gentleness, becomes so palpably real that he can almost be seen and touched. The narrative technique of the story is simple and perfectly suited to the deep simplicity of Rosicky's character. His story fulfills Willa Cather's criterion of a truly great story, which "must leave in the mind of the sensitive reader an intangible residuum of pleasure; a cadence, a quality of voice that is exclusively the writer's own, individual, unique."[1]

"Old Mrs. Harris," completed in 1931, was probably begun during the last months of Mrs. Cather's illness. Though the setting is Skyline, Colorado, and some of the background material fictionalized, the core of the story is derived from Willa Cather's family. Old Mrs. Harris (for whom the prototype was Willa Cather's Grandmother Boak) seems to the town of Skyline to be the Templeton family drudge, unused as that western community is to the Southern custom in which every young married woman has an older

* Page references in this discussion are to *Obscure Destinies* (New York: Alfred A. Knopf, 1932).

woman who keeps in the background and manages the
household. With five children in her daughter's family
and very little money, things are much harder for Mrs.
Harris than they had been back home in Tennessee,
but she considers it right and natural to preserve her
position in the kitchen so that her handsome daughter,
Victoria, can also preserve hers in the parlor.

Mrs. Harris is old and tired, but she lives for her
family. Her prime concern is deflecting the good-inten-
tioned efforts of the neighbors to pay to her the attention that she feels should be paid to Victoria, and in
keeping her family from realizing how old and tired
she indeed is. In this latter concern she has little difficulty: the four younger children see their grandmother
simply as an untiring source of love and comfort; Victoria and her oldest daughter, Vickie, are absorbed in
their own compelling concerns. Vickie needs three
hundred dollars beyond her scholarship to cover her
college expenses, and her father is unable to give it to
her. Mrs. Harris, though her strength is failing, determines to do something that is very hard for her: she
asks their neighbor Mrs. Rosen if her husband can lend
Vickie the money she needs. Vickie gets the loan,
though without knowing of her grandmother's part in
it, and is so immersed in her preparations to go away
that she has no thought of anyone else.

At the same time Victoria learns to her dismay
that she is pregnant again. She locks herself in her
room to nurse her resentment at life, which has not
treated her as she expected it would when she married.
With the household in this state of crisis, no one but
Mandy, the mentally retarded servant, notices that
Mrs. Harris is failing, and only the younger children
are there to sit by her bed and read to her. Mrs. Harris

is convinced that she will die during the night and is humbly thankful that she will be able to die without troubling anybody.

A longer and technically more complex story, "Old Mrs. Harris" is very different in style from "Neighbour Rosicky." Yet at its core Willa Cather has again created a flawless characterization of a selfless and loving human being, one quite different from Rosicky and uniquely herself, a humble, self-effacing old woman whose presence is evoked beyond any physical description and whose solidity and depth are unquestionably real. Though as a work of art the story is complete and needs no commentary as to its meaning, Willa Cather made its message explicit in old Mrs. Harris's words, unthinkingly released from deep within her, when her grandson begs to know the reason for the suffering of his dying cat: "Everything that's alive has got to suffer" (p. 141). She is happy and at peace with herself and is able to die well because she has learned this truth and accepted it; she has even accepted the unthinking self-absorption of the young who have not yet learned it. Willa Cather closes the story with this comment:

Thus Mrs. Harris slipped out of the Templeton's story; but Victoria and Vickie had still to go on, to follow the long road that leads through things unguessed at and unforeseeable. When they are old, they will come closer and closer to Grandma Harris. They will think a great deal about her, and remember things they never noticed; and their lot will be more or less like hers. They will regret that they heeded her so little; but they, too, will look into the eager, unseeing eyes of young people and feel themselves alone. They will say to themselves: "I was heartless, because I was young and strong and wanted things so much. But now I know" [p. 190].

The last story in the collection, "Two Friends,"
is a fictionalized account of Willa Cather's memories of
the sidewalk conversations of two of her father's friends
in Red Cloud. In the story the two friends are R. E.
Dillon, the principal banker and proprietor of the
general store, and J. H. Trueman, a big cattleman.
The young narrator admires them because they are
secure and established, as contrasted to the "nervous
little hopper men" who are trying to get on, and
because theirs was the only real "conversation" that
could be heard in the town. Dillon, the younger of the
two, is a more dramatic personality, with a touch of
the reformer's zeal; Trueman is more conservative and
stolid. Their friendship is destroyed when Dillon, a
Democrat, backs the free-silver candidacy of William
Jennings Bryan, for which Trueman has nothing but
contempt. Though the characterizations and some of
the descriptive passages are very fine, the story lacks the
full emotional realization of "Neighbour Rosicky" and
"Old Mrs. Harris." It remains a sketch, important less
for what it evokes in its own right than for what it
represented to its author: "the feeling of something
broken that could so easily have been mended; of
something delightful that was senselessly wasted, or a
truth that was accidentally distorted—one of the truths
we want to keep" (p. 230).

13

Lucy
Gayheart
(1935)

In some aspects of its plot, *Lucy Gayheart* is reminiscent of *The Song of the Lark*. Like Thea, Lucy is a small-town girl who goes to Chicago to study music; but while Thea's desire is for artistic creation itself, Lucy finds the embodiment of her desire in the person of the singer Clement Sebastian, whose rehearsal accompanist she becomes. When he hears of the death of his one-time closest friend, Sebastian comes to realize the emptiness of his life and the irrevocable loss of his youth. In this void Lucy's spirit and vitality, and her idealistic and unselfish devotion to Sebastian, seem to be like "springtime coming in at the door" (p. 89).* For Lucy, Sebastian makes real the intangible yearnings she has always felt:

How often she had run out on a spring morning . . . in pursuit of something she could not see, but knew! It was there, in the breeze, in the sun; it hid behind the blooming apple boughs, raced before her through the neighbours' gardens, but she could never catch up with it. Clement Sebastian had made the fugitive gleam an actual possession. With him she had learned that those flashes of promise could come true, that they could be the important things in one's life. He had never told her so; he was, in his own person, the door and the way to that knowledge [pp. 183–84].

Meanwhile, Harry Gordon, the richest young man in Lucy's home town of Haverford, situated on the Platte, has decided to sacrifice his ideas of making a socially important marriage in order to marry Lucy, who is only a watchmaker's daughter but who has something about her that no other girl has. Coming to Chicago in the midst of Lucy's idyll with Sebastian,

* Page references in this discussion are to *Lucy Gayheart* (New York: Alfred A. Knopf, 1935).

Harry takes her out to dinner and announces his intention of marrying her. He is indulgently amused
when she tells him she loves another man, and in order
to make him take her feelings seriously, she furiously
tells him that she and Sebastian are having an affair.
Harry thereupon walks out on her, leaving her to get
home from the restaurant as best she can.

Shortly after this Sebastian leaves for a European
tour, planning to return in the autumn. In September
he is drowned in a boating accident, and Lucy, completely broken up, returns to Haverford. There she
tries to get Harry to speak to her, wanting simply to
be friends with him and believing he is cold to her
because of her supposed affair with Sebastian. But
Harry, who had promptly married a socially prominent
woman in order to spite Lucy, feels that Lucy should
be punished for what she has made him do, and he
treats her with impersonal remoteness.

Lucy drags herself dispiritedly through the autumn. Just before Christmas she attends a performance
of *The Bohemian Girl,* in which a worn old soprano
who still sings with intelligence and understanding re-
awakens something in her. She begins to feel she wants
to go back to Chicago and take up her life and her
music again. She wants again all the beauty she had
known with Sebastian, but does not yet know how she
can do it alone. Then she has a stunning realization:

What if—what if Life itself were the sweetheart? It was like
a lover waiting for her in distant cities—across the sea. . . .
Oh, now she knew! She must have it, she couldn't run away
from it. She must go back into the world and get all she
could of everything that had made him [Sebastian] what he
was. Those splendours were still on earth, to be sought after
and fought for. In them she would find him. *If with all your*

heart you truly seek Him, you shall ever surely find Him. He had sung that for her in the beginning, when she first went to him. Now she knew what it meant [pp. 184–85].

Unable to return to Chicago until March, Lucy frets away the days in Haverford, where there is nothing to match her new enthusiasm for life. One day, after a quarrel with her sister, she rushes out of the house with her skates to the old skating place on the river. On the road she meets Harry Gordon coming along in a sleigh and asks him for a ride. He refuses, saying he is late for an appointment and she will take him out of his way. Blinded with anger and pain, Lucy strides furiously to the river and launches out on the ice, not knowing that skating there is no longer safe since the river changed its course the preceding spring. The ice breaks, the water is deep, and Lucy drowns.

The last section is a long epilogue focusing on Harry Gordon twenty-five years after Lucy's death. His actions during those years have had a certain unpredictability, indicating that after all there is more to him than the veneer of the successful banker which he presents to the world. He has gotten over his guilt at Lucy's death and has come to feel that she is "the best thing he had to remember" (p. 223), the only uncommonplace human being he had known. Lucy and her gift of joy, of being "wildly happy over trifling things," take their place in his memory "along with all the fine things of youth, which do not change" (p. 224).

Lucy Gayheart reflects Willa Cather's lifelong concern with the "invisible, inviolable world" (p. 104), the reality of which is intuitively sensed in childhood and, in adulthood, is apprehended in art or religion. Lucy seems to represent the thrust toward that world, the desire itself, seen like a meteor momentarily flashing across the sky and then extinguished. In contrast to Lucy's momentary brightness (even her name means light) is the commonplace world of Haverford. The most outstanding representative of this world is Harry Gordon, who, though he loves Lucy for her impulsiveness and *joie de vivre,* would not choose to be like her if he could. The novel simply presents and contrasts these two figures, the one seeking the inexpressible splendor of life, the other satisfied to pursue mundane triumphs. It is an exercise in statement rather than development. Though it is not a bad novel, it is curiously lifeless and lacks the evocative quality which characterizes Willa Cather's best fiction.

14

The Old

Beauty,

and Others

(1948)

"The Old Beauty," the title story in this collection, is set in Aix-les-Bains, France, in 1922. The story is seen through the eyes of fifty-five-year-old Henry Seabury, an Anglo-American who has just returned from a long business career in China to find with disappointment how the Western world has changed during his absence. Aix-les-Bains, however, is still "more or less as it used to be" (p. 7).* Here he meets an old woman whom he had known in his youth as Gabrielle Longstreet. Her name recalls for those who remember it "a society whose manners, dress, conventions, loyalties, codes of honour, were different from anything existing in the world today" (p. 5). Now her beauty is gone, her health is poor, and she is living in seclusion and anonymity with a companion, the former music-hall comedienne Cherry Beamish. Gabrielle has nothing but contempt for the modern era and modern manners. She cherishes the memories and photographs of the great men who were her friends in her youth and whose true greatness she has only been able to recognize now that they are gone and there are no others like them.

Seabury, some fifteen years younger than Gabrielle, seems to regard the great figures of the past with something of the same admiration that he accords Gabrielle, and she takes great pleasure in his company. One day, returning from a drive to the mountains, their car is forced off the road in order to avoid hitting a car driven by two young American flappers. Gabrielle is badly shaken by the sudden stop and suffers severely from the presence of the swaggering and impertinent girls, whom Seabury, with polite disgust, finally sends on their way. The next morning Gabrielle is dead.

* Page references in this discussion are to *The Old Beauty, and Others* (New York: Alfred A. Knopf, 1967).

The tone of the story is very much Gabrielle's tone of severity and coldness toward a world from which she no longer expects either recognition or consideration. As an evocation of the feelings of Gabrielle, a beautiful ornament of London society of the 1890s who has outlived her time, it is undeniably powerful, but the feelings it evokes are not pleasant. Many critics have tended to see this story as an expression of Willa Cather's own antagonism to the present and therefore use it in support of their interpretation of her as a grim and embittered old woman resembling Gabrielle. This, I think, is unjustified. While Willa Cather presents the plight of Gabrielle Longstreet in terms of the old beauty's negative reaction to the present, she also provides a foil in the person of Gabrielle's companion, Cherry Beamish. Cherry is described as vigorous, plump, a "most comfortable little person" whose presence considerably warms the chilly atmosphere Gabrielle creates and who finds the present "really very interesting, if only you will let yourself think so" (p. 31). While it is Gabrielle's story and Gabrielle's mood that dominates it, Cherry's cheerful presence suggests that it is not also Willa Cather's story and mood. It is, rather, a portrait of a woman and her feelings, somewhat reminiscent of the portrait of Marian Forrester in *A Lost Lady*: Mrs. Forrester was also a beauty who outlived her time and suffered in her own way because of its passing, as Gabrielle Longstreet suffered in her way.

"The Best Years," the second story in the collection, grew out of Willa Cather's childhood memories of her family. The core of the story is the deep love between sixteen-year-old Lesley Ferguesson and her four younger brothers. All of the circumstantial details

—Lesley's teaching at a country school, which requires her to board away from home; the visit from the county superintendent of schools, Miss Knightly, which makes possible Lesley's surprise visit home; the small, cramped, but beloved house; the foolish, impractical father to whom the children are unanimously loyal; the handsome mother, who manages on her husband's inadequate income—all these details serve to create and make substantial the feelings Lesley experiences in the heart of her family:

> Lesley sank down on the porch floor, her feet on the ground, and sank into idleness and safety and perfect love.

> The boys were much the dearest things in the world to her. To love them so much was just . . . happiness. . . . sitting in the warm sun, with her feet on the good ground, even her mother away, she almost ceased to exist. The feeling of being at home was complete, absolute: it made her sleepy [p. 112].

Lesley dies of pneumonia the following winter. Twenty years later Miss Knightly (now Mrs. Thorndike) makes a visit to Mrs. Ferguesson. The boys are grown and gone, and Mr. and Mrs. Ferguesson now have a new and spacious house. But their new prosperity does not compare, in Mrs. Ferguesson's mind, with all the happiness they had in the old house, when the family was together and completely absorbed in the day-to-day attempts to make ends meet: "Well, this I know: our best years are when we're working hardest and going right ahead when we can hardly see our way out" (p. 136).

"Before Breakfast," the last story in *The Old Beauty, and Others,* presents an interesting thematic contrast to "The Best Years." Whereas in "The Best

Years" the focus is on Lesley's joyous loss of herself in her love for her family, "Before Breakfast" deals with a man who has kept the core of his inner self private. Henry Grenfell, the senior partner of the bond house of Grenfell and Saunders, has worked hard all his life. He has married well and raised three sons, who, though successful, are cold as ice. Grenfell's one escape from his business and his family is his cabin on a remote island off the coast of Nova Scotia. The rugged, isolated island is more than a refuge for Grenfell; he loves it, and feels a deep relationship with it. Now, en route to the island, he meets a professor of geology, who innocently tells him of the island's great geologic age. Grenfell, the humanist, is staggered, and spends a bad night. He finds the incommensurability between geologic time, measured in millions of years, and mere human experience to be thoroughly unsettling: "A man had his little hour, with heat and cold and a time-sense suited to his endurance. If you took that away from him you left him spineless, accidental, unrelated to anything" (pp. 148–49).

Going out for a walk before breakfast, Grenfell encounters the simple sensuous beauty of the woods and cliffs and realizes that after all nothing has changed; he has always known that the rock must be ancient, but "that fact had nothing to do with the green surface where men lived and trees lived and blue flags and buttercups and daisies and meadowsweet and steeplebush and goldenrod crowded one another in all the clearings" (p. 161). Looking over the edge of the high cliff, he sees the geologist's daughter stepping out of her white bathrobe in order to go for a cold swim. She is wearing a pink bathing suit, and she makes him think of a little pink clam opening its white shell. At first he is annoyed with her for her foolhardiness in swimming out into the cold North Atlantic, and wonders how he can get down to the narrow beach to rescue her. Then she returns to shore, and his mental scolding turns to acknowledgement of her pluckiness; she had done what she had set out to do, with no fuss. Grenfell returns to his cabin in good spirits; the geologic ages behind him no longer bother him, and he delights in the girl's plucky youth, suggestive of the eager ongoingness of life.

Though the subject is lightly treated in an ironic, whimsical tone that exactly matches Grenfell's character, the place of man in a universe of incomprehensible age and vastness is a serious question to which Willa Cather has given a serious answer. Grenfell's anguish at his own absurdity in the face of the "merciless perfection, ageless sovereignty" of Venus, the morning star, is real enough, though it is carefully understated. Also understated is the simple reestablishment of his relation with nature through his early morning walk and his vision of the girl, whose unconscious attitude is so suggestive of Botticelli's "Birth of Venus." Where much of modern literature, dealing with this same question, has found only alienation and despair, Willa Cather reaffrms the reality of relationship.

15

A Final Word:
Other Views
on Willa Cather

The British critic David Daiches, who published the first book-length study of Willa Cather after her death, noted the difficulty of appraising her work:

There are few writers of her distinction whose achievement is so difficult to sum up. She belongs to no school. . . . she cannot be helpfully classified with respect to either theme or technique. . . . But the reader of her best novels is not likely to worry about that. These novels have a strength and an individuality that it is not easy for the critic formally to describe, virtues which can be experienced even if they cannot easily be talked about. Her position among American novelists is unique; no other has brought to bear quite her kind of perception on the American scene.[1]

E. K. Brown, who wrote the standard critical biography of Willa Cather, linked her with the great symbolist writers:

Her vision is of essences. In her earlier novels the essential subject, a state of mind or of feeling, was enveloped in the massiveness of the conventional modern realist novel. It was there, but it was muffled. Then she saw that if she abandoned the devices of massive realism, if she depended on picture and symbol and style, she could disengage her essential subject and make it tell upon the reader with a greater directness and power, help it to remain uncluttered in his mind. The things that pass, the things that merely adhere to states of mind and feeling, she began to use with a severe and rigid economy. Her fiction became a kind of symbolism, with the depths and suggestions that belong to symbolist art, and with the devotion to a music of style and structure for which the great literary symbolists strove. . . .[2]

Edward A. and Lillian D. Bloom placed Willa Cather's work at the heart of the American literary tradition:

136

More notably even than Cooper, and with a moral intensity comparable to that of Hawthorne, Melville, and James, Miss Cather has represented the tensions of American existence in the late nineteenth and early twentieth century. Like her predecessors—especially the last three—she is a commentator on the prevailing American condition. Sometimes urgent in her fears but always ardent in her faith, she constantly held before herself the vision of realizable ideals. Out of inspired singleness of conviction grew a distinguished art.[3]

The writer Katherine Anne Porter made the penetrating observation that Willa Cather's provinciality, far from being a liability, is the source of her art. Miss Porter linked her not only with her great American predecessors but with some of the great European novelists:

Mr. Maxwell Geismar wrote a book about her and some others called *The Last of the Provincials*. Not having read it I do not know his argument; but he has a case: she is a provincial; and I hope not the last. She was a good artist, and all true art is provincial in the most realistic sense: of the very time and place of its making, out of human beings who are so particularly limited by their situation, whose faces and names are real and whose lives begin each one at an individual unique center. Indeed, Willa Cather was as provincial as Hawthorne or Flaubert or Turgenev, as little concerned with aesthetics and as much with morals as Tolstoy, as obstinately reserved as Melville. In fact she always reminds me of very good literary company. . . . She is a curiously immovable shape, monumental, virtue itself in her work and a symbol of virtue—like certain churches, in fact, or exemplary women, revered and neglected.[4]

Dorothy Van Ghent summed up Willa Cather's achievement:

Willa Cather's stature as a novelist and storyteller will probably always withstand those obscurations which happen to a
major writer almost with the regularity of the displacement
of one generation by another; for her best work reaches into
human truths immeasurably older than the historical American past from which she drew her factual materials, truths
that provide the essential forms of experience and that
therefore cannot become "past" truths, either obsolescent or
elegiac. . . . For the same reason, the dense world of the
five senses which she creates in her best novels and stories is
one that cannot be interpreted by an abstraction (a "world-
view" of some kind); her work rests on an intuitive or instinctive wisdom, conveying "a direct and untranslatable
message" like old Rosicky's gypsy hand, or like the image
of the black plow picture-written on the molten sun. What
she did was very difficult, for she had to give up conventional literary methods, in which she was accomplished, and
go blindly into herself for essential truth. Yet it was through
that giving up and blindness that she was able to speak in a
way that often reveals to the reader something extraordi-
narily valuable that seems to have been in his mind always.[5]

Notes

An Overview

1. Lionel Trilling, *After the Genteel Tradition* (New York, 1937). Excerpt quoted in James Schroeter, ed., *Willa Cather and Her Critics* (Ithaca, New York: Cornell University Press, 1967), p. 153.
2. James Woodress, *Willa Cather: Her Life and Art* (New York: Pegasus, 1970), p. 187.
3. Alfred Kazin, *On Native Grounds* (New York, 1942). Excerpt quoted in Schroeter, *Willa Cather and Her Critics*, p. 164.
4. Ibid., p. 170.
5. Ibid., p. 168.
6. Miguel de Unamuno, *Tragic Sense of Life* (New York: Dover Publications, Inc., 1954), p. 321.
7. Henry Steele Commager, *The American Mind* (New Haven, Conn., 1950). Excerpt quoted in Schroeter, *Willa Cather and Her Critics*, p. 209.
8. Unamuno, *Tragic Sense of Life*, p. 321.

1. Willa Cather's Life

1. Bernice Slote, ed., *The Kingdom of Art: Willa Cather's First Principles and Critical Statements 1893–1896* (Lincoln: University of Nebraska Press, 1966), p. 13.

2. Ibid., p. 295.

3. Edith Lewis, *Willa Cather Living* (New York: Alfred A. Knopf, 1953), p. 53.

4. Willa Cather, *Alexander's Bridge,* new edition with preface (Boston: Houghton Mifflin Co., 1922), p. v.

5. Ibid., p. viii.

6. Sarah Orne Jewett quoted in Lewis, *Willa Cather Living,* pp. 66–67.

7. Elizabeth Shepley Sergeant, *Willa Cather: A Memoir* (Lincoln: University of Nebraska Press, 1963), p. 80.

8. Willa Cather, *On Writing* (New York: Alfred A. Knopf, 1949), p. 79.

9. Willa Cather, *Not under Forty* (New York: Alfred A. Knopf, 1936), p. 63.

10. Ibid., pp. 76–77.

11. Ibid., p. 79.

12. Ibid., p. 77.

13. Ibid., p. 80.

2. *O Pioneers!*

1. Elizabeth Shepley Sergeant, *Willa Cather: A Memoir* (Lincoln: University of Nebraska Press, 1963), p. 85.

2. Willa Cather, *On Writing* (New York: Alfred A. Knopf, 1949), p. 92.

3. Ibid.

4. Ibid.

5. *See* Mircea Eliade, *The Sacred and the Profane* (New York: Harper Torchbooks, 1961), p. 31.

3. *The Song of the Lark*

1. E. K. Brown, *Willa Cather: A Critical Biography* (New York: Alfred A. Knopf, 1953), p. 186.

5. *My Ántonia*

1. James E. Miller, Jr., *"My Ántonia:* A Frontier Drama of Time," *American Quarterly* 10, no. 4 (Winter 1958):476.
2. Mircea Eliade, *The Sacred and the Profane* (New York: Harper Torchbooks, 1961), pp. 12, 28.
3. Ibid., p. 10.

7. *A Lost Lady*

1. Joseph Wood Krutch, in *Nation,* 28 November 1923. Excerpt quoted in James Schroeter, ed., *Willa Cather and Her Critics* (Ithaca, New York: Cornell University Press, 1967), p. 52.
2. Willa Cather, *Not under Forty* (New York: Alfred A. Knopf, 1936), pp. 48–49.

8. *The Professor's House*

1. Elizabeth Shepley Sergeant, *Willa Cather: A Memoir* (Lincoln: University of Nebraska Press, 1963), p. 215.
2. Willa Cather, *On Writing* (New York: Alfred A. Knopf, 1949), pp. 31–32.
3. Ibid., p. 32.
4. Leon Edel, *Willa Cather: The Paradox of Success* (Washington, 1961). Excerpt quoted in James Schroeter, ed., *Willa Cather and Her Critics* (Ithaca, New York: Cornell University Press, 1967), p. 269.
5. Ibid., p. 267.
6. Carl G. Jung, *Psyche and Symbol* (Garden City, New York: Doubleday Anchor Books, 1958), p. 133.
7. Ibid., p. 135.
8. Ibid., p. 144.
9. Ibid., p. 136. The italics are Jung's.

9. *My Mortal Enemy*

1. Willa Cather, *Not under Forty* (New York: Alfred A. Knopf, 1936), p. 51.
2. Ibid.
3. Richard Giannone, *Music in Willa Cather's Fiction* (Lincoln: University of Nebraska Press, 1968), p. 175.

10. *Death Comes for the Archbishop*

1. Willa Cather, *On Writing* (New York: Alfred A. Knopf, 1949), p. 10.
2. Clinton Keeler, "Narrative without Accent: Willa Cather and Puvis de Chavannes," *American Quarterly* 17, no. 1 (Spring 1965):126.
3. Ibid.
4. *See* Mircea Eliade, *The Sacred and the Profane* (New York: Harper Torchbooks, 1961). Mircea Eliade uses "religious" to mean "one open to an awareness of the sacred," and in this sense Alexandra and Ántonia and Jim Burden, as well as Father Latour and Father Vaillant, can be described as religious.
5. Cf. ibid., p. 167.
6. Cf. ibid., p. 48.
7. Ibid., p. 65. Italics are Eliade's.
8. Cf. ibid., pp. 73ff.
9. The suggestions of the evolutionary development of man as a species is curiously akin to the thought of Pierre Teilhard de Chardin. *See especially The Future of Man* (New York: Harper Torchbooks, 1969).
10. In the twentieth-century development of psychoanalysis the recovery of one's personal past (the forgotten contents of the unconscious) can be seen as regenerative or redemptive. Eliade sees a connection between the interest in one's personal origins in psychoanalysis and

archaic man's concern with primordial time and the
origins of the cosmos. *See* Eliade, *Myth and Reality*
(New York: Harper and Row, 1963), pp. 77ff.
11. From the sixteenth-century series of woodcuts by Hans
Holbein called *The Dance of Death*.

12. Obscure Destinies

1. Willa Cather, *On Writing* (New York: Alfred A. Knopf,
1949), p. 50.

15. A Final Word: Other Views on Willa Cather

1. David Daiches, *Willa Cather: A Critical Introduction*
(Ithaca, New York: Cornell University Press, 1951), pp.
186, 189.
2. E. K. Brown, *Willa Cather: A Critical Biography* (New
York: Alfred A. Knopf, 1953), p. 340.
3. Edward A. and Lillian D. Bloom, *Willa Cather's Gift
of Sympathy* (Carbondale: Southern Illinois University
Press, 1964), p. 239.
4. Katherine Anne Porter, *The Days Before* (New York:
Harcourt, Brace & Co., 1952), pp. 72–73.
5. Dorothy Van Ghent, *Willa Cather,* University of Minnesota Pamphlets on American Writers, no. 36 (Minneapolis: University of Minnesota Press, 1964), p. 44.

Bibliography

1. Works by Willa Cather

Alexander's Bridge. Boston: Hougton Mifflin Co., 1912.

April Twilights. Boston: Richard Badger, 1903.

Collected Short Fiction 1892–1912. Edited with an introduction by Mildred R. Bennett. Lincoln: University of Nebraska Press, 1965.

Death Comes for the Archbishop. New York: Alfred A. Knopf, 1927.

The Kingdom of Art: Willa Cather's First Principles and Critical Statements 1893–1896. Edited with two essays and a commentary by Bernice Slote. Lincoln: University of Nebraska Press, 1966.

A Lost Lady. New York: Alfred A. Knopf, 1923.

Lucy Gayheart. New York: Alfred A. Knopf, 1935.

My Ántonia. Boston: Houghton Mifflin Co., 1918.

My Mortal Enemy. New York: Alfred A. Knopf, 1926.

Not under Forty. New York: Alfred A. Knopf, 1936.

O Pioneers! Boston: Houghton Mifflin Co., 1913.

Obscure Destinies. New York: Alfred A. Knopf, 1932.

The Old Beauty, and Others. New York: Alfred A. Knopf, 1948.

On Writing. With a Foreword by Stephen Tennant. New York: Alfred A. Knopf, 1949.

145

One of Ours. New York: Alfred A. Knopf, 1922.

The Professor's House. New York: Alfred A. Knopf, 1925.

Sapphira and the Slave Girl. New York: Alfred A. Knopf, 1940.

Shadows on the Rock. New York: Alfred A. Knopf, 1931.

The Song of the Lark. Boston: Houghton Mifflin Co., 1915.

The Troll Garden. New York: McClure, Phillips & Co., 1905.

Willa Cather in Europe. Edited by George N. Kates. New York: Alfred A. Knopf, 1956.

The World and the Parish. Willa Cather's Articles and Reviews, 1893–1902. Selected and edited with a commentary by William M. Curtin. 2 vols. Lincoln: University of Nebraska Press, 1970.

Youth and the Bright Medusa. New York: Alfred A. Knopf, 1920.

2. *Works about Willa Cather*

Bennett, Mildred. *The World of Willa Cather.* New edition with notes and index. Lincoln: University of Nebraska Press (Bison Books), 1961.

Bloom, Edward A. and Lillian D. *Willa Cather's Gift of Sympathy.* Carbondale: Southern Illinois University Press (Arcturus Books Edition), 1964.

Brown, E. K. *Willa Cather: A Critical Biography.* New York: Alfred A. Knopf, 1953.

Daiches, David. *Willa Cather: A Critical Introduction.* Ithaca, New York: Cornell University Press, 1951.

Giannone, Richard. *Music in Willa Cather's Fiction.* Lincoln: University of Nebraska Press, 1968.

Lewis, Edith. *Willa Cather Living.* New York: Alfred A. Knopf, 1953.

Randall, John H., III. *The Landscape and the Looking Glass: Willa Cather's Search for Value.* Boston: Houghton Mifflin Co., 1960.

Schroeter, James, ed. *Willa Cather and Her Critics.* Ithaca, New York: Cornell University Press, 1967.

Sergeant, Elizabeth Shepley. *Willa Cather: A Memoir.* Lincoln: University of Nebraska Press, 1963.

Van Ghent, Dorothy. *Willa Cather,* University of Minnesota Pamphlets on American Writers, no. 36. Minneapolis: University of Minnesota Press, 1964.

Woodress, James. *Willa Cather: Her Life and Art.* New York: Pegasus, 1970.

Index